THE Teenage Entrepreneur's Guide

50 money-making business ideas.

Sarah L. Riehm

SURREY BOOKS
101 East Erie Street
Suite 900
Chicago, Illinois 60611-2811

To the teenagers of Plano, Texas, and the New Horizon.

THE TEENAGE ENTREPRENEUR'S GUIDE is publishd by Surrey Books, 101 E. Erie St., Suite 900, Chicago, IL 60611. Telephone: (312) 751-7330.

This book was manufactured in the United States of America.

2nd edition. 1 2 3 4 5

Library of Congress Cataloging-in-Publication Data

Riehm, Sarah L., 1952–
  The teenage entrepreneur's guide.

  Includes index.
  1. Youth—Employment—United States. Self-
employed—United States. I. Title.
HD6273.R53   1987   658'.041   87-1904
ISBN 0-940625-00-8

Single copies may be ordered from Surrey Books for $12.95 (check or money order) postpaid. For quantity discounts, please contact the publisher.

Book design by Joan Sommers Design, Chicago
Cover design by Hughes Design, Chicago
Editorial production by Bookcrafters, Inc.

Acknowledgments

Since the first edition of this book was printed, I have had the opportunity to meet many teenagers who are accomplishing amazing things with their lives. I've met teenage inventors, tycoons and business leaders all across the country. For example, one young man built a multi-million-dollar telemarketing business before the age of twenty. A young woman patented a game that is distributed nationwide. A ghetto teenager, finding no opportunities in the job market, set up a successful catering business that now employs 30 people. And these kids aren't just making money; they are having fun in the process.

The point is, kids everywhere have really picked up on the entrepreneurial spirit. Schools have begun to respond to this increased interest in entrepreneurship. According to *USA Today*, "40% of the nation's high schools have begun weaving entrepreneurial instruction into vocational classes. Another 10% offer specific courses in how to start and run a company."

This second edition is dedicated to those inspiring young people who have demonstrated the main theme of this book: almost anything is possible if you set your mind to it. It is also dedicated to the next generation of enterprising entrepreneurs.

Preface

What Your Parents Will Want to Know About This Book

The teenage years are a time when everything seems possible—or everything seems just beyond reach. Today's parents are too often tempted to smooth the path for their children, to hand them everything they need and more, to solve all their problems. Today's kids *need* to be challenged, to test their mettle, to find out who they really are. Meaningful work provides the ultimate testing ground. Starting a small business is an excellent way to discover self-worth at an early age. Teenagers have the chance to try something on their own, independent of the sometimes overwhelming pressure of peers and family members. In work, kids learn how to strive for important goals, to cope with real problems. Running a business instills the maturity to face issues head-on and find solutions. Work teaches decision-making skills that carry over into every aspect of life. The teenager with experience making important decisions is better equipped to deal with the problems and pressures of modern teenage life.

Many parents worry about conflicts between a teenager's work and school. This book is geared to the full-time student. It does *not* advocate leaving school to work. It stresses the value of education, and how work can help fulfill long-term educational goals. The fifty business ideas in this book are all intended to be run as part-time ventures requiring less than twenty hours of work per week, and are flexible enough to be scheduled around a busy student's school activities. In fact, the teenager running his or her own business is more likely to be able to juggle school and work responsibilities than the teen working for an employer.

You won't be alone in running a part-time business. Entrepreneurship among teens is rising rapidly. Although exact figures aren't known, government statistics show that one-third of all new businesses are started by people under the age of thirty. Verne C. Harnish, director of the Association of Collegiate Entrepreneurs, says, "The young entrepreneur is emerging as this generation's hero."

One distinct advantage for teens starting their own business is that the experience can be a valuable ticket for getting into the college of their choice. A few years ago, top-level schools selected students primarily on the basis of outstanding grades and test scores. However, times are changing. The September, 1986, issue of *Money* magazine reports that "Admission directors . . . are drawn to resourceful applicants who find ways to distinguish themselves from the crowd." Topping the list of admission fast tracks is starting a small business. According to the *Money* report, the teenage entrepreneur demonstrates superior leadership and initiative. Even students with somewhat weak academic skills but attractive qualities "stand a much better chance of getting in at many of the most popular schools than those with B's and no extra features."

For students who have no college ambitions, starting a business provides a tremendous headstart in the business world. Many teen entrepreneurs discover a part-time business during their high school years that they can turn into a full-time profession after graduation.

Bill Cunningham, a Texas teen, started a telemarketing business while still in high school. By the time he was eighteen, he was running a multi-million-dollar telemarketing corporation. He has been featured on several national television programs and in 1987 was one of nine recipients of *Venture* magazine's "Entrepreneur of the Year" awards.

Even a small business that ends in failure is better resume material than sacking groceries for the summer. Running a venture gives a teen first-hand experience in the essential aspects of business. Such experience during the school years can be invaluable in making that first major career choice after graduation.

The fifty ideas in the *Teenage Entrepreneur's Guide* are relatively low risk and simple to manage. Even if a teen fails in starting a business, he or she gains insight that will bring success to future endeavors. If that first business is a success, the teenager takes a tremendous leap toward financial independence and the responsibilities and rewards of an adult career.

Contents

Ideas for picking up extra cash around holiday time

The Teenage Entrepreneur— How to Earn Money on Your Own

So you want to make some money! Who doesn't? *But how?* If you have surveyed the current job market, prospects look dim. The national unemployment rate right now is between 5 and 6 percent. But for young people in some large cities, it runs well over forty percent. You have probably checked out the "teen jobs" in your area, such as sacking groceries and flipping hamburgers. Usually the pay isn't great and the hours can conflict with school activities. Baby-sitting, cutting grass, doing a few odd jobs around the neighborhood—if you have tried any of these, you probably know that the pay is usually a lot less than minimum wage, and the work doesn't provide a steady income.

Jobs outside the neighborhood require reliable transportation not available to many teens. To get a car to drive to your job would eat up most or all of your wages. Plus, most good jobs require experience. Employers won't hire you unless you have it, and you can't get it until you are hired. It's a vicious circle.

Fifty Business Ideas

What other choices do you have? Plenty. The best choice of all is to be your own boss. This book will demonstrate how any teenager can set up his or her own serious, professional part-time business. The fifty business ideas presented in this book:

▶ Are flexible enough to schedule around your school activities.

▶ Can generate at least minimum wage.

▶ Will provide you with a steady part-time income.

▶ Can teach you valuable business skills that can turn your venture into a successful full-time career, or help you in future business activities.

▶ Can be run out of your home.

▶ Require little or no expertise, capital or transportation.

Advantages of Being an Entrepreneur

If you are interested in becoming an entrepreneur, you must have drive, determination and discipline. You will have to work hard—perhaps harder, at first, than if you were working for someone else. But there are tremendous advantages to having your own business:

▶ You are free to determine your own schedule.

▶ You don't have to take orders from anyone except your customers.

▶ You are free, within reason, to set your own wages.

▶ Your earnings are limited only by your own drive and determination.

▶ You have a tremendous opportunity to learn the ropes of the business world at an early age.

▶ You can make new friends and contacts who can help you in future endeavors.

▶ MONEY! Money for savings, clothes, a car, stereo, dates, or for the best investment of all, your education.

The World of Business

Running your own company introduces you to all the business basics. It also gives you an opportunity to understand in greater depth than most teens how the business world works, and how American business interacts with government, the community, and society in general.

The Teenage Entrepreneur's Guide provides you with an introduction to the four basic building blocks of business:

Management   **Marketing**   **Finance**   **Accounting**

1. Management In business, management is leadership. As an entrepreneur, you are the one in control of your business destiny. Management tips are included throughout this book, but most of the basics are reviewed in Chapter 3, Step-by-Step Approach to Setting Up Your Own Business. As a manager, your tasks are to:

Plan for your business, from preparing a beginning strategy to making daily decisions affecting its future.

Analyze what your customers really need, and how best to meet those needs.

Control your business, from cutting costs to increasing profits.

Organize your work, your resources and time so that you use them efficiently and meaningfully.

2. Marketing Peter Drucker, the American dean of management science, defines marketing in this way:

> Marketing is so basic that it cannot be considered a separate function. . . . It is the whole business seen from the point of view of its final results, that is, from the customer's point of view.

Each of the fifty business ventures in this book includes marketing ideas. Chapter 5, Marketing Tips, provides an overview of marketing promotion.

Your tasks as a marketing manager are these:

▶ To design the best possible product or service to meet your customer's needs.

▶ To set a price for your products high enough that you earn a decent profit, but low enough to attract customers.

▶ To communicate with your prospective customers through advertising, personal selling and promotion techniques to build your business.

3. Finance Finance is the realm of money and banking. Most of the ventures in this book don't need money to start with—sometimes called "start-up capital." However, Chapter 3 gives you some fund-raising suggestions. As a business owner, you'll most likely need the services of a local banker. Banking services are described in Chapter 3.

4. Accounting Accounting is keeping track of the general health of your business. Accounting activities include:

▶ Keeping detailed records of your business costs and income.

▶ Preparing tax returns for federal, state and local governments.

▶ Preparing reports that track your financial progress over time.

▶ Organizing business records in an orderly way.

Accounting and bookkeeping requirements are discussed in Chapter 6, and Chapter 7 includes a description of tax reporting.

The World of the Teenage Entrepreneur

Being a young entrepreneur brings its own set of possibilities, rewards and problems. Your age and inexperience can be handicaps in the competitive environment of business, but enthusiasm, drive and a little advance planning can overcome most problems.

The entrepreneur faces an added element of uncertainty, of risk. If you need a steady, predictable, sure thing, then being an entrepreneur isn't for you. You will have to deal with some or all of the following problems. Fortunately, each has a solution.

Problem: Fear of losing money
Solution: Minimize investment

Many entrepreneurs stay awake at night worrying about losing money. Therefore, most of the ideas in this book are designed to be set up with little or no money. The few materials required could be easily used around the house or sold. If you make any money at all, you'll be ahead of the game.

Problem: Conflict with school activities
Solution: Flexible schedules

This book is intended for full-time junior and senior high school students who put school first. Therefore, all the ideas are intended to be after-school, part-time ventures. They are flexible enough to work around any reasonable schedule of classes and extra-curricular activities. However, if you want to be a serious entrepreneur you will have to set up a regular time to conduct your business activities. You will have to make sacrifices and skip some school events, as does anyone trying to pursue important goals outside of school.

Problem: Conflict with family members
Solution: Be considerate and professional

Running a business out of a busy household can create conflicts. Be considerate of your family. Don't expect them to pitch in and help you for free. Don't take advantage of Mom or Dad. If you are planning to use something of theirs in your business, at least volunteer to pay them for it. If your business runs up their utility bills—say, if you were regularly washing cars or doing laundry in your home—try to determine what portion of the utility bill belongs to you. Take responsibility for it and pay your fair share. If your phone starts ringing off the wall with orders for your new business, consider putting in your own private line.

Problem: Fear of failure
Solution: Understand that just *starting* a business is an outstanding achievement

Failure really means failure to try. If you try, then you are already well down the road to success. Remember the old saw "Nothing ventured, nothing gained"? You might worry about what your friends will think if you start your own business. It may not be what they consider the normal thing to do. You might worry about embarrassment if you fail. No new business venture can get off the ground without sweat, toil and some major glitches. You *cannot* find a successful person in business today who has never experienced failure. To become a great person, you must learn somewhere along the way to deal with and overcome adversity. Think about what failure means to you. Success for the entrepreneur means the ability to earn money, without having to punch someone else's time clock.

How to Avoid the Three Biggest Mistakes

There are three major reasons that most new businesses fail.

1. Undercapitalization—or lack of money to keep the business going—is number one. New business owners often fail to understand the amount of cash required to set up and operate a new venture. *Most of the ideas in this book require little, if any, beginning investment.* If you do select a business venture requiring more cash than you have on hand, check the fund-raising suggestions in Chapter 3.

2. Lack of publicity/advertising Many new businesses suffer from a shortage of customers. The ideas presented in this book are mostly service businesses; you can expect to get enough customers right in your neighborhood to keep you busy part-time. Refer to Chapter 5 for tips on getting noticed. Building a clientele (a set of customers) takes hard work, a lot of hustle, and doing a great job for existing clients. Word-of-mouth recommendation by satisfied customers is the most reliable and cheapest form of advertising.

3. Failure to understand the market Many eager entrepreneurs throw themselves into a marketplace where there are already too many competitors. Or they don't understand who needs their product and why. Either mistake can spell doom. The demand is booming for most of the service businesses outlined in this book. However, look before you leap. Check out the competition. Determine whether your service or product is new to your area. If so, you have a tough job. You have to convince your neighbors they need something new, and that will take product education. Do some trial marketing

5

by checking with neighbors and friends about their willingness to buy your service.

Dealing with Rejection

Good salespeople always anticipate what to do with rejection. Because you are young, you will get plenty of it. Here are listed some of the most common reasons people will give you for not buying your service or product, and how to overcome them:

Rejection: You don't have enough experience!
Counterattack: Offer something special to balance your lack of experience. One or all of the techniques listed below can counteract inexperience.

▶ Set your prices significantly lower than your competition's.

▶ Study your competition and your customers. Offer something special that your customers will value – and that your competitors do not provide.

▶ Your more established competitors may have become complacent. They may not take enough time with their customers. You may get the business just by demonstrating that you are more eager, more willing to work and better able to satisfy your customers. After all, you are their neighbor, not a stranger they might select out of the telephone book.

▶ Have a list of good references handy. If you haven't established business references yet, ask a neighbor, pastor, or teacher to be ready to give your prospective clients a glowing character reference. Or, offer to provide cut-rate service for a few of your neighbors in return for a good reference if you do a good job. Be sure to ask permission ahead of time if you want to use someone as a reference.

▶ To satisfy your more stubborn clients, guarantee your results; satisfaction or their money back. Be prepared to back up your promise with excellent performance.

Rejection: You will be here today and gone tomorrow! Teenagers don't stick with anything.
Counterattack: This is a common complaint, not without reason. The fact is, you are probably intending your business to be temporary, to earn money for college or the next step in your career. Try to impress potential customers with your

professionalism. Dress neatly. A business card and snazzy advertising and brochures help put customers at ease (see Chapter 5). Also, if you are planning to run your business for only a short time, say for your junior and senior years, plan to have a younger friend in the neighborhood take over for you in the future. Make your clients aware of your junior partner. They'll be more willing to buy from you if they are convinced the business will be around for the long term.

Rejection: I just don't need what you're selling!

Counterattack: This rejection may come up because customers don't understand your product or service. Make sure your advertising adequately explains what you have to offer. Some people really do need the service, but they may want to do some comparison shopping. If you have direct competition, be sure to have their prices handy. If you can beat your competition's price and demonstrate that to your prospective customer, you are likely to get the business. If you handle rejection poorly, pick a business idea that doesn't require much direct selling. For example, all you need to make a good living in the latchkey, laundry or housecleaning business is one or two regular customers. Of course, if a customer really doesn't need what you have to offer, there's not much to be done.

Boost Your Chances for Success

What are some of the things you need to know beforehand that can boost your chances for success? Here's a short checklist that can improve your odds:

1. Check the competition first.

You are going to be the new kid on the block. If you want to succeed, you must offer a better deal: more service for less money. Check out all your competitors. You should be completely familiar with what products and services they provide and at what price. Have that information available for your prospective clients, or publish price comparisons in your advertising.

2. Investigate the business thoroughly.

Go through the steps outlined in Chapter 3. Don't skip any of them. If you think they are too much hassle, then you probably don't have what it takes to run a business of your own.

3. Understand your costs.

Most of the ideas in this book don't require much cash up front. However, draw up a list of everything you think you might need. If you have some competition, try to check out what tools and equipment they are using. Don't overdo it! It's easy to find customers if you spend a lot of your own money on fancy equipment to impress them. Successful entrepreneurs are the ones who keep as keen an eye on trimming costs as on raising revenue.

4. Your main job is to sell yourself.

No matter what it is you are trying to sell, your primary job is to SELL YOURSELF! How can you convince people to buy from you if they don't like or trust you? Try these sure-fire techniques.

Before the sale:

▶ Conduct yourself in a professional manner. Take yourself and your customers seriously.

▶ Dress neatly. Wear a uniform, such as a polo or T-shirt with your company name on it, whenever possible.

▶ Have references ready.

▶ Be friendly, relaxed, confident!

▶ Treat everyone with courtesy and gratitude. If you respond courteously to a rejection, it may turn into a future sale.

▶ Make sure your products and pricing are consistent. If you make a special introductory offer to one first-time client, carry the policy across the board. You don't want a prospective client to get wind of a special "deal" for the neighbor next door that isn't available to him.

After the sale:

▶ Always be on time.

▶ Have a trained substitute ready for emergency situations when you can't make an appointment. Don't make a habit of missing appointments, though!

▶ Make sure you have all the required equipment on hand and organized before you get to your customer's home.

▶ Thank customers for their business—more than once.

▶ Make sure clients are satisfied with your service. Ask them for suggestions for improvement.

▶ Follow up every satisfied customer appointment with a request to schedule a repeat visit. YOUR BEST BUSINESS PROSPECTS ARE YOUR OWN SATISFIED CUSTOMERS!

Have Fun!

Another key to success is to pick a business that you can enjoy. These ideas will keep the fun in your work:

1. Don't pick something over your head. For example, don't plan on giving piano lessons if you didn't get past basic training. Consider the physical requirements of the job. Can you lift and transport all the equipment necessary? If you pick a job that requires transportation, do you have a reliable vehicle?

2. Don't pick something that is more trouble than it is worth. The fifty jobs described in this book are all intended to earn at least the minimum wage. Don't burn yourself out working for less than $3.50 an hour. You will get frustrated and angry; it will be a waste of your time. For example, many people love to work with crafts. But they may underestimate the time involved, and they don't or can't charge enough to cover their labor. Say you love to knit Christmas stockings. You notice the mail order catalogs sell them for $25. You feel confident you can sell nicer ones you make yourself. You price yours at $15, which you feel is as much as you could possibly charge. Yet you know it takes twenty hours to knit one sock. Even though you feel $15 is expensive, you would be earning less than $1 per hour! It doesn't matter how much you love to knit. If you get an avalanche of orders, after a while you will resent the fact that you are working for slave wages.

3. Determine whether you like to work alone or with others. That is a very critical business decision. Sometimes it's fun to have a friend along. Cleaning a house can go more quickly with company, but it cuts into your profits if your friend or partner slows down your work.

4. Be super organized. The mechanics of running a business can get to be a hassle. Keep all your forms, records and papers filed so you can retrieve them quickly. Keep an appointment book with you at all times. Organization is the best way to prevent the little things from getting you down.

5. Pick a viable business idea, one that will work for you in your own community. Give it your best shot, but if after a reasonable length of time, say six months, it doesn't take off, pick another business idea. Sometimes, even the best idea offered by the best person cannot be successful. Analyze your reasons for failure. Was it you? Lack of interest or dedication? Or was it the marketplace? Too much competition? Or not enough customers to support the business? If you are convinced you have given it your best shot and you still don't achieve a reasonable income, try something else. If you learn that you have no talent for entrepreneurship, you may have saved yourself from a greater financial disaster down the road. And you certainly will have acquired a greater understanding of who you are.

The Rewards Make It All Worthwhile!

Now you know some of the rewards of—and problems with—being your own boss. The biggest reward is in the long term. Running a small business can teach you important lessons: struggling with adversity, dealing with people quite different from yourself, coping with success. As a young entrepreneur, you will be much better equipped to deal with real life as an independent person; real life where your parents and friends won't be around to bail you out of every difficulty. As an entrepreneur, you will be tested as an adult, not as a child, every day. This testing will produce a stronger, confident, more successful YOU!

2

What Makes a Successful Entrepreneur?

There's no doubt that entrepreneurial fever is sweeping the land. In a recent issue of *Money* magazine, managing editor Landon Jones reports, "Suddenly, exhilaratingly, entrepreneurship is in the air." But just what does the word "entrepreneur" mean?

The word was coined around the year 1800 by French economist J. B. Say. The term today means someone who starts and runs his or her own *new* and *small* business. It is the person who creates something from nothing. For some, entrepreneur means a person who takes daring risks. The news concentrates on flamboyant risk-takers, such as Stephen Jobs, who founded Apple Computers and most recently the NeXT computer company, or that kingpin of wheeler dealers, Donald Trump. However, in many cases starting up your own venture needn't be riskier than starting any other occupation.

Experts seem to be divided on what it takes to be a successful entrepreneur. Half the experts believe entrepreneurs are BORN, not made. Researchers spend a great deal of time trying to prove that certain personality traits destine a person to become an independent business owner. Other writers believe that entrepreneurs are MADE, not born. Peter Drucker writes in *Innovation and Entrepreneurship:*

> [Entrepreneurship] is not a personality trait; in thirty years I have seen people of the most diverse personalities and temperaments perform well in entrepreneurial challenges. To be sure, people who need certainty are unlikely to make good entrepreneurs. . . . Everyone who can face up to decision making can learn to be an entrepreneur and to behave entrepreneurially. Entrepreneurship, then, is behavior rather than a personality trait.

Richard Eisenberg, a writer for *Money* magazine, agrees. "If I came away with any one certainty about who can become an entrepreneur in America, it is that anyone can."

Despite this attitude, universities and research centers all across America still try to discover the secrets of successful entrepreneurs. Many studies have established a relationship between certain character traits and the successful entrepreneur. Research indicates that entrepreneurs:

1. Are driven by a need to achieve.
2. Have a great desire for recognition.
3. Possess an extremely high energy level.
4. Are task-oriented. They are "doers" rather than "thinkers."
5. Choose a challenge over security.
6. Can recognize a profitable opportunity.
7. See opportunity where others do not.
8. Have a high level of self-confidence.

The research doesn't seem to jibe with other experts' opinions that anyone can be an entrepreneur. Are entrepreneurs born, or made? The truth lies somewhere in the middle. If you are a shy, retiring type who is chronically depressed and only gets things done after constant nagging by a parent or teacher, then the entrepreneur route is probably not for you. Do you have what it takes?

The following test should help you decide if being an entrepreneur is for YOU! It measures your EQ, your *E*ntrepreneurial *Q*uotient. The questions are designed to see how well-equipped you are to handle the business ventures described in this book, and are meant especially for teenagers who will be running small businesses out of their homes. Take time to answer each question thoroughly and sincerely. The answers will help you assess your overall business potential. First, answer each question by checking Y ☐ yes, or N ☐ no. Then, follow up by filling in the blank below each question.

The Teenage Entrepreneur's EQ Test

☐ Y ☐ N 1. Do you set long-term goals (longer than six months) for yourself and follow through to complete them? List some of your major long-term goals below:

_____   _____

_____   _____

☐Y ☐N   2.   Do you normally finish school and/or home assignments without prodding from parents or teachers? List some of those assignments you have successfully completed recently:

_____   _____

_____   _____

_____   _____

☐Y ☐N   3.   Do you work well by yourself? List some things you like to do when you are alone.

_____   _____

_____   _____

_____   _____

☐Y ☐N   4.   Have you had experience earning and saving money? Briefly describe your savings history. Include the amounts you currently have in the bank, when you started saving, and sources of income.

_____

_____

_____

_____

☐Y ☐N   5.   When you are with your friends, are you a natural leader? For example, do your friends regularly look to you for guidance and advice, or have you been elected an officer of any club or organization? List your leadership roles below:

_____   _____

_____   _____

_____   _____

_____   _____

☐Y ☐N   6.   Do you have at least ten hours a week of spare time you can devote to a small business? Draw up a sample schedule for one of your typical weeks, day by day. Using the form below, list the hours you already spend on classes, homework, TV, dates, extra-curricular activities, mealtime, etc. Then, show where you have EXTRA time available, at least ten hours, for running a business.

	MON	TUE	WED	THU	FRI	SAT	SUN
7 AM							
8 AM							
9 AM							
10 AM							
11 AM							
NOON							
1 PM							
2 PM							
3 PM							
4 PM							
5 PM							
6 PM							
7 PM							
8 PM							
9 PM							
10 PM							

☐Y ☐N 7. Do you keep your school and personal records in good order? For example, do you keep close track of your homework assignments or social schedule with an appointment calendar or datebook?
Describe the elements of your life you like to keep organized, and what methods you use to do it. _____
_____
_____

☐Y ☐N 8. Have you achieved success in other areas of your life—good grades, music, athletics, scouting, community service, etc.?
List your achievements below: _____
_____
_____

☐Y ☐N 9. Have you ever planned and successfully completed a major project on your own? (A fund-raising project, soap box for the derby, science fair project, scouting award, scout cookie drive, 4-H or FFA project, a large-scale gardening project, etc.)
Briefly describe the project(s) below, including a description of how long each took, and how successful you thought you were: _____

_____

_____

_____

☐Y ☐N 10. Do you like to dream up new ideas? Have any of these ideas been implemented by friends, family or organizations you belong to?
List some of the good ideas you have come up with lately:

_____

_____

_____

☐Y ☐N 11. Do you like to compete? (For example, athletics, debate, music, 4-H.)
List below the areas of your life in which you compete, and how well you think you do:

_____   _____

_____   _____

_____   _____

☐Y ☐N 12. If you are currently working for somebody else, are you dissatisfied with your job or the way things are run?
Describe what you would change about your current job and why.

_____

_____

_____

☐Y ☐N 13. Are you confident and usually successful when asking people for help, money or support?
Briefly list the situations where you have had to ask people

for money or favors, such as selling tickets, school fund-raising projects, etc. How successful were you?

_____

_____

☐Y ☐N 14. When you tackle a project, do you budget enough time to complete it, so you don't face last-minute crises?
Can you think of any recent projects, such as school papers, you missed the deadline on? List those projects below, and try to analyze why you were late in finishing them.

_____   _____

_____   _____

_____

☐Y ☐N 15. Do you usually show up for activities on time, and is being prompt important to you?
Think about all the regularly scheduled events you go to: school, church, job, etc. For what percentage of these events are you on time?

_____

☐Y ☐N 16. Do you have a stable and *reasonably* quiet home environment, one that allows you to carry out tasks that require concentration (such as homework)?
If you have serious household disruptions that currently interfere with your homework, what could you do to improve the situation?

_____

_____

_____

☐Y ☐N 17. Do you relate well to adults; for example, do you have any adults you regularly rely on for advice?
List their names below:

_____   _____

_____   _____

_____   _____

☐Y ☐N 18. Do you think you have a lot of friends and acquaintances in your community, school and neighborhood? List some of the key people who might be helpful to you in starting your business: (A banker, church leader, attorney, class officer, business leader, etc.)

_____   _____

_____   _____

_____   _____

☐Y ☐N 19. Do you have a set of financial goals? If you earn money in your business, do you have a good idea what you will use it for?
List below your financial goals, what you want to buy and how much it will cost:

_____   _____

_____   _____

_____   _____

☐Y ☐N 20. Have you ever worked for wages before? Describe your job responsibilities below, and how well you think you did in that job(s): _____

_____

_____

Interpreting the Results

The questions above cannot absolutely predict your success or failure in running a business of your own, but they are a fairly good indicator of how well equipped you are to run a teen enterprise. How well did you do? Check your score below. Give yourself one point for every YES answer.

_____ **Write your total score here**

0 to 5 points	You should think twice about starting your own business.
6 to 10 points	You have a fair chance of success, but you will have to learn a lot in order to succeed.
11 to 15 points	You have a good chance of success. You have a solid background of experience and knowledge. Analyze your "NO" answers to find room for improvement.

16 to 20 points You have the potential to be a business superstar. Your well-rounded background should equip you nicely for managing a small business of your own.

Analyzing Your Answers

If you answered "YES" to a majority of the questions on the test, you can feel confident about starting a small business on your own. While this in and of itself cannot guarantee financial success, the above questions pinpoint the strengths of a true entrepreneur. You might want to discuss your answers with your parents or another adult advisor. The paragraphs below analyze the importance of each of the questions on the test to your success at a new business venture:

Question 1. Setting goals and developing a plan to achieve those goals is probably the most important key to success. Entrepreneurs must understand what success in their business means, and how to achieve it. You need to analyze not only your goal-setting abilities, but your ability to follow through to completion. Lots of teens are enthusiastic and set many ambitious goals and projects for themselves, but burn out before they have finished them.

Question 2. Entrepreneurs need to be able to accomplish goals on their own, without prodding or nagging. Your past track record on school assignments should be a good indicator of how well you could do on your own.

Question 3. The entrepreneur must develop plans with little or no help from others. If you cannot or don't like to work by yourself, you might be happier working for other people.

Question 4. One of the requirements of setting up a business is that you understand the basics of money management. Every business requires recordkeeping and banking activities. While these can be learned, you'll have a giant headstart if you already have some experience managing money.

Question 5. Knowing how to lead others and how to influence decisions is important to most entrepreneurial ventures. You must be able to convince customers to trust in you and your products or service in order to earn money. If you take a back seat in your circle of friends, letting others make the decisions and set the rules, you might not have the self-confidence to sell yourself to prospective customers.

Question 6. You must have AT LEAST ten hours a week of spare time to run your own business, and probably more in the beginning. If you are already swamped with school and social activities, then think twice about taking on a project of this magnitude. You'll be setting yourself up for failure. If you can't identify at least ten available hours for your new business venture, and you still want to earn money, analyze which of your activities you would be willing to drop or cut back on.

Question 7. Running a business takes self-discipline to manage the small things. You must be able to keep track of schedules, customers, costs and profits. This takes proper attention to detail. The big-scale entrepreneur can afford to hire someone to keep track of things. You cannot. Check around your room at home. Are you always losing important papers? Can't keep track of appointments? If so, you'll have to change your ways and learn to manage YOURSELF better if you want to succeed in managing a business.

Question 8. Looking at your past successes is a good indication of how important achievement is to you. Almost all serious research on entrepreneurs says they crave achievement and recognition—far more than money! If achievement alone doesn't motivate you, you might not have the "stick-to-itiveness" to keep going on your own.

Question 9. Have you planned and completed any major projects on your own—perhaps a science fair project, a soap box for the derby, a major scouting badge, a fund-raising drive for charity? If so, you already understand the types of activities necessary to start and run a business.

Question 10. The entrepreneur must be something of a dreamer, an idea generator. Contrary to popular belief, you don't have to dream up a brand-new, earthshaking idea to build a successful business. But you *do* need to have some original ideas about solving problems and promoting yourself and your products.

Question 11. If you hate competing with other people, you might not be happy as an entrepreneur. You will have to compete every day where it really counts—in the marketplace, with your own money, time and resources.

Question 12. Research shows that most entrepreneurs strike out on their own either because 1) they disliked working for others—just didn't fit in—or 2) felt that, wherever they were working, they could do the job better than their coworkers or boss. This dissatisfaction is something more than the usual complaints about low wages or bad hours typical of teen jobs. Do you regularly have specific gripes and ideas on how to improve your work situation?

Question 13. If you are going to run your own business, you will be constantly asking people to do things for YOU, to buy your products, to help out, to give you money. If you are shy about these things, you won't get very far.

Question 14. Running a business takes some smarts about scheduling your own activities. You need a good feel for how long it takes you to complete a wide range of activities. If you constantly underestimate how long it takes to do things, you will get in immediate trouble in business facing disappointed clients when you can't meet your commitments.

Question 15. Promptness doesn't always count, but in most of the business ventures in this book, you must be on time to satisfy your customers. Your clients need to know they can count on you. One of the best indicators of your reliability is if you show up when you SAY you will, and finish promptly.

Question 16. The business ventures described in this book are intended to be run out of your home. You will need a quiet place to work, to receive phone calls, to keep orderly business records. If you live with constant turmoil and emotional disruptions in your household, it might seriously affect your ability to get your job done. For some teens, however, household problems can be a motivating factor to work extra hard. Sit down and carefully analyze your ability to get work done at home. If you think it's impossible, perhaps you could arrange to work out of somewhere else–a friend's house, the church. You could even consider renting a small cubicle with an answering service at a secretarial services company, which could cost anywhere from $30 a month on up. However, any of these alternatives will be a handicap over operating out of your own home. If you are experiencing real household problems–such as alcoholism, drug abuse, physical or verbal abuse–consider seeking professional help from your school counselor, pastor or community social services bureau.

Question 17. Virtually all the business ideas in this book require you to work with adults–as customers, advisors or business associates. If you can't *stand* working with anyone "over the hill," you may be headed for trouble. Running your own business doesn't shield you from the world of adults. However, it does put you on a more equal footing with them.

Question 18. Having a wide circle of friends and acquaintances is one of your best assets going into a new business. You'll need to tap all of your contacts in developing a list of customers.

Question 19. You should have a firm idea what you are working *for*. Financial goals provide motivation to work and earn money over the long haul. If you are working simply to earn money for more clothes, more pizza, more movies, more dates, you may quickly realize the hard work isn't worth it. Having some long-range, serious goals such as college, a car or moving out on your own makes your work meaningful and worthwhile.

Question 20. Work experience is no guarantee that you will do well in a business of your own, but you have a leg up on those who have never worked. You already understand the basic responsibilities involved, such as being on time, looking nice for work, being reliable. Running your own business magnifies those responsibilities.

Where to Go for Help

If you want to learn more about being an entrepreneur, the following books may help you:

Charlotte Taylor, *The Entrepreneurial Workbook* (New York: New American Library, 1985)

Peter F. Drucker, *Innovation and Entrepreneurship* (New York: Harper and Row, 1985)

James R. Cook, *The Start-Up Entrepreneur* (New York: Truman Talley Books, E. P. Dutton, 1986)

Also, check the many interesting and informative books about entrepreneurship written by Joseph Mancuso.

The Small Business Administration (SBA) was set up by the federal government to help people just like you. Though the future of the SBA seems cloudy (the current government budget crisis threatens to cut back the SBA's activities or shut it down altogether), at present, it is still alive and operating. The SBA offers a wide range of pamphlets and services. Some are free, some are very moderately priced. SBA pamphlets cover a wide range of topics, from *Financial Recordkeeping* to *Starting and Managing a Small Business of Your Own* to *What is the Best Selling Price?*. Contact your nearest SBA office for a list of publications and services. For a small charge, they will send you Document 115A, listing 130 or so current publications. If you can't locate one of the SBA's 106 regional offices, call the head office in Washington toll-free at 1-800-368-5855 for the nearest office and phone number.

Most communities offer seminars and courses on entrepreneurship. A short, three-hour course should give you all the basics and strengthen the concepts presented in this book. Check with your local community college, extension service or Chamber of Commerce to see what's available.

Many schools have clubs or organizations especially for teens interested in business and entrepreneurship. If you'd like to belong to a business organization, the following provide excellent training and support for their members. If you can't find a local chapter, contact their national headquarters listed below for further information:

1. Junior Achievement
Phone: 719-540-8000

Address: 45 East Clubhouse Drive
              Colorado Springs, CO 80906
Goal: To help kids understand business and the
              economy.

2. Future Business Leaders of America
Phone: 703-860-3334
Address: P.O. Box 17417-Dulles
              Washington, DC 20041
Goal: To help the individual gain the self-
              confidence, leadership and business skills
              necessary for today's business environment.

3. Busines$ Kids
Phone: 1-800-852-4544 (toll-free)
Address: 301 Almeria Avenue, Suite 330
              Coral Gables, FL 33134
Goal: To introduce young people to the American
              system of free enterprise, and to help them
              set up a profitable business of their own.

Step-by-Step Approach to Setting Up Your Own Business

This book is for the teenager who wants to set up and manage a *real* business. Many teens do earn money on their own, of course. Countless teens cut grass, baby-sit, or perform odd jobs around the neighborhood. However, the vast majority don't treat this work as a *business*. They don't do any serious marketing to help their earnings grow, they don't keep financial records, and they don't file income tax returns. Usually, conducting business this way isn't very profitable; besides, it is downright *illegal*. You are obligated by federal law to keep business records and report any earnings from self-employment over $400 per year.

This chapter demonstrates, step by step, how to set up a small business. It's not difficult! It just takes a little time and planning before you open up shop. There are many benefits to setting up a "real" business, as opposed to earning a little money under the table. Starting a small business:

▶ Gives you great experience—experience you can use to get a job in the future, to gain admission to the college of your choice, or to start a career that could last a lifetime.

▶ Teaches you things you can't learn in school. Most important, it gives you a special EDGE, a real head start on life beyond school.

▶ Offers greater earning potential than doing odd jobs or working in a fast-food restaurant.

The business ideas in this book are intended to be operated in the simplest way possible. In order to keep it simple, your business should be set up:

1. As a SOLE PROPRIETORSHIP (see definition below),

2. Using very SIMPLE ACCOUNTING techniques,

3. Without hiring any EMPLOYEES,

4. With little or no START-UP CAPITAL (beginning investment money) required,

5. And operated out of your OWN HOME.

1. There are three types of business entities: the sole proprietorship, the partnership, and the corporation. A sole proprietorship is a business owned by ONE person (regardless of how many employees are working in it). The many advantages of keeping strictly to the SOLE PROPRIETORSHIP form are:

▶ There's no need for complicated legal documents. Both partnerships and corporations require complex paperwork and expensive legal advice.

▶ You don't have to prepare difficult tax returns.

▶ You can start and stop your business whenever you please.

▶ Recordkeeping is simple.

(NOTE: It's usually not necessary or an advantage to the sole proprietor to form a corporation until annual earnings are over $100,000.)

2. Most large businesses use very sophisticated accounting systems. They also can afford to hire an army of accountants. This is totally unnecessary for you. The simpler, the better. Elementary recordkeeping, as described in Chapter 6, should meet your needs.

3. The business ideas described in this book don't require you to hire any employees. Hiring help really complicates things. As an employer, the government says you must withhold taxes, file extra forms, pay social security and unemployment taxes. Plus, preparing payroll checks is a big hassle.

4. Most of the business ideas in this book don't need much, if any, start-up capital. The majority of them can be managed on a shoestring budget. You won't be applying at a bank for business loans. This is beyond the capability of most teenagers.

5. The businesses in this book can be run out of your own home easily. You'll need a quiet, organized place to keep your business records, and you'll need access to a telephone. You *won't* need fancy office space, secretarial services or office equipment.

The Step-by-Step Approach

Successful entry into the business world requires a few simple steps. The most important thing to remember is that *it's not too difficult!* Anyone can set up a business. Just follow these steps before you start, and you're on your way to *success!*

Step 1 Read this book *entirely.*

Step 2 Select a business venture that's right for you.

Step 3 Prepare a simple business plan.

Step 4 Register with the appropriate government agency(ies).

Step 5 Set up a simple recordkeeping system. (See Chapter 6.)

The next two steps aren't always necessary. Whether you need them depends on the business you select. The instructions for Steps 6 and 7 are provided later in this chapter.

Step 6 Set up a bank account.

Step 7 Raise money.

Step 1 Read This Book Entirely

Before you decide whether you *want* to be an entrepreneur, read this book all the way through. By the time you finish, you'll have a complete picture of all the activities required to be your own boss.

Step 2 Select a Business Venture

This is perhaps the most important thing for you to decide. Pick a business you will enjoy and for which you're suited. How do you pick one that's just right? Check the list below. After reading through all the Fifty Ideas, come back to this section to help select the one for *you.*

▶ **Pick a business right for your *age.*** Many of the business ideas are suitable only for older teens. They require strength or expertise beyond the capability of those under sixteen, or require the ability to drive. Some ventures particularly suited to younger teens are:

no. 3	Recycling	**no. 23**	Home Bakery
no. 4	Neighborhood Directory	**no. 24**	Buttoneer
no. 5	House Numbers	**no. 33**	Handicrafts
no. 17	Super Baby Sitter – Special Afternoons	**no. 41**	Personalized Greeting Cards
no. 18	House Sitting		

▶ **Select a business you will *enjoy!*** If you hate math, even if you get good grades in math, don't set yourself up as a math tutor. Even if there's a great need for math tutors, if you don't like it, you won't do a good job at it, and probably won't be able to stick with it very long.

▶ **Select a business you can perform well.** Practice a few times before you actually go into business. For example, if you select Idea #20, Window Washing, practice around your own house. Ask others to evaluate your work. Some people don't have the muscular strength or patience to do a good job. If you want to give lessons, you must have truly superior ability and a track record of public achievement. For example, if you want to teach piano, you should have some clearly demonstrated ability, such as contest awards or experience accompanying the school or church choir.

▶ **Select a business that's right for your community.** Most of the ideas are suitable for the average town, suburb or big city. Only you can decide what's right for your own community. For example, if you live in a tiny town in rural Minnesota where most women work as homemakers, your chances for earning much money cleaning houses are small. You won't earn vast amounts with a swimming pool service in Wyoming. If you live in the country, you might earn quite a bit painting fences, but don't expect to cash in with a neighborhood directory or word processing service. The best indicator of what will work is to see what's being offered in your community. Usually, your best opportunities are in businesses that are *already* in your town; people are familiar with that type of business. If that business is successful, chances are, you will be, too.

▶ **Select a business right for your personality.** Do you like working by yourself, in a quiet atmosphere? Then you might pick cleaning houses or window washing. Do you like being a ham? Try #31, Clowning Around, or #45, Chauffeur Service. Do you feel confident about meeting people? Are you a born salesperson? Then sell products door to door, or at school.

Step 3 Prepare a Simple Business Plan
The next step in setting up your business is putting together a basic business plan. It doesn't need to be fancy, but you

must make your best estimate of the costs involved and the profits you expect *before you start your business.* The business plan will do the following:

▶ It will help determine if you can earn at least minimum wage in your new business. If not, you're better off working for someone else.

▶ If you do need to borrow a small sum of money for start-up costs, it will demonstrate to your lender your ability to pay back the loan.

▶ It will give you a concrete set of goals to work toward.

Follow through these simple steps to arrive at *your* basic business plan. Then, put the whole plan together on the worksheet included on page 36.

First: Decide on a time period.

Second: Set up a work schedule.

Third: Estimate your costs.

Fourth: Establish your price(s).

Fifth: Estimate how much business you expect.

1. Decide on a time period. When are you planning to start up your business? How long do you plan to continue your business? Just for next summer? Your senior year? The next three years? Or do you plan on turning this into a full-time occupation? For planning purposes, remember that any business requires at least one month of planning and organization before you open the doors to your customers. For example, if you want to paint houses for a summer, you'll need to get organized in April and May. **My business time period will be** (fill in below):

_____

_____

2. Set up a work schedule. You've already thought about this if you filled out the "EQ" test in Chapter 2. Now, go back and fine-tune that schedule. See if it makes sense with the business you've selected. How many hours a week do you have for work? Be realistic. You need to have at least *ten* free hours. But you can't cut out mealtimes, homework time, sleeping, etc. Don't forget that every working person needs free time every week just for play or relaxation. In other words, you can't schedule every waking hour. Determine the *maximum* hours you can work. If you are going to school full-time, your maximum work time shouldn't exceed twenty hours per week during the school year.

3. Estimate your costs. Some of the ideas in this book don't involve any costs at all, such as #32, Giving Lessons. If so, go to the next section.

Business costs can be divided into two types: FIXED and VARIABLE.

▶ **Fixed costs** These are costs unrelated to the number of customers you have—in other words, materials and equipment needed to run day-to-day business operations. Examples of *fixed* costs are start-up expenses such as office supplies, equipment, telephone installation, answering machine, or a desk. You may experience other *fixed* costs during the course of running your business, such as ongoing advertising expenses, telephone bills, and office supplies. The easiest way to estimate ongoing *fixed* costs is to budget a set amount per month.

My fixed costs will be:

A. Start-up expenses:

Item	Cost
_____	$_____
_____	_____
_____	_____
_____	_____
_____	_____
_____	_____
_____	_____
_____	_____

Total start-up costs: $_____

B. Other fixed expenses (estimate a monthly amount):

Item   Cost per month

_____ $_____

_____   _____

_____   _____

_____   _____

_____   _____

_____   _____

_____   _____

Total other fixed expenses $___ per month

▶ **Variable costs** These are costs that vary depending upon the number of products you sell or the number of customers you have. For example, if you are washing cars, you'll use a certain amount of supplies per car wash, such as two capfuls of soap, a rag or two, and wax. If you use a power tool to buff the wax, this isn't really a VARIABLE cost, but a FIXED cost. You will buy it or borrow it when you start business. Its cost does NOT vary depending upon how busy you are.

My variable costs per product or per customer will be:

Item   Cost

_____ $_____

_____   _____

_____   _____

_____   _____

_____   _____

_____   _____

_____   _____

_____   _____

_____   _____

_____   _____

_____   _____

Total variable costs $_____

4. Establish your price(s). There are two methods to set a fair price for a product or service.

▶ **Method One:** Base your price on the competition. Call around to all your competition to see what they're charging, and exactly what they offer for the price. Because you are new, inexperienced and want to build a business fast, you should set your price significantly lower than your competition, so that your customers can clearly see that you have bargain rates. Your price should be at least twenty-five to thirty percent less than your professional, established competition. If you find that you can't undercut your competition without working for slave wages, consider another business.

Example, using Method One
Giving Lessons, Idea #32

The going rate in your town for piano lessons is $9 per half hour. You decide to charge $5, to entice new customers with your bargain rates.

▶ **Method Two:** The second method is based upon your costs, and how much you want to earn per hour. Follow these steps to arrive at a price:

Step 1. How much do you want to earn per hour?

$_____ per hour

Step 2. Exactly how long does it take you to make your product or perform your service for each customer? You should *always* practice a few times to verify your time estimate.

_____ hours per product/customer

Step 3. What are your total *variable costs* per product or customer? (Check back to your estimates from the previous page.)

$_____ per product/customer

Step 4. Now, multiply your hourly wage from Step 1 by your time estimate in Step 2, then add in your *variable costs* in Step 3. That should bring you to a total price:

	Time estimate:	_____	hours per customer
×	Wages:	$_____	per hour
=	Total wages:	$_____	
	Plus add in:	$_____	Total VARIABLE COSTS
	EQUALS:	$_____	FINAL PRICE

Example, using Method Two:
Auto Detailing, Idea #1

Step 1. You want to earn $6 per hour.

Step 2. It takes you three hours to do a thorough job of washing, waxing and finishing a car.

Step 3. Your material costs per customer are $1.00 for disposable rags, a capful of detergent, plus ¼ jar of car wax.

Step 4.

	Time estimate:	3	hours per customer
×	Wages:	$ $6	per hour
=	Total wages:	$ 18	
	Plus add in:	$ 1	VARIABLE COSTS
	EQUALS:	$ 19	FINAL PRICE

Method Two should work *unless:*

▶ Your final price comes up too high compared with the competition. If it does, either you are taking too long to perform the task or your wage expectations are unreasonably high. If you can't cut your time down, you may have to accept a lower hourly wage. If this doesn't work, you might want to pick another business venture.

▶ You have a lot of *fixed* costs. If so, you'll have to increase your price to cover them.

5. Estimate how much business you expect. This last step is usually the most difficult, because you have to do some educated guesswork. You'll need to estimate how many products or customers you expect to sell every month. Here are some tips to help you do the estimates:

▶ Don't expect to sell at full capacity right from the start. Be conservative when estimating sales in the first few months, unless you already have a large volume of business lined up before you begin.

▶ Don't forget that any business has to make seasonal sales adjustments. Unless you are selling holiday-related services or products, business will probably drop off during December. If you are washing cars in a cold climate, don't estimate high sales volume during the winter months.

▶ Remember to schedule some vacation time. You might want time off for exam week, spring break, Christmas, or family vacations.

▶ Determine how many hours per week you want to work. Don't estimate more sales revenue than this work week maximum will support, unless you have partners or hire helpers.

Example
Giving Lessons, Idea #32

You want to estimate your first year's earnings, using the following assumptions: You will start your business in January. You already have three students lined up. You don't want to teach more than ten hours per week, or twenty total students. You wish to take three weeks off during the Christmas holidays, one week for Easter, and one week during August for a summer vacation. Your price will be $5 per half-hour lesson.

Business Plan
Jan Smith's Piano Lessons

Month:	Jan	Feb	Mar	Apr	May	Jun	Jul	Aug	Sep	Oct	Nov	Dec
Lessons per month	12	20	32	48	56	64	80	60	80	80	80	20
$ per month	$60	100	160	240	280	320	400	300	400	400	400	100

($5 per lesson)

That is a total of 632 lessons in the first year. 632 times $5 per lesson is $3160 total revenue for the year.

Before you construct your own business plan, follow through the example below for Tim's Housepainting Service:

Sample Business Plan
For Tim's Housepainting Service

First: Decide on a time period.

Tim plans on housepainting full-time for the next summer only. He will start lining up customers in April. In May, he will purchase all his supplies and organize his schedule. By the first of June, he expects to have a summerful of clients already lined up, and will begin painting. He'll finish at the end of August.

Second: Set up a work schedule.

His work schedule will be forty hours per week, from eight a.m. to four p.m. Monday through Friday.

Third: Estimate your costs.

Tim's costs are:

Fixed costs

A. Start-up expenses

Professional heavy-duty paint sprayer	$160
Door-to-door flyers for advertising	20
Miscellaneous painting supplies (scrapers, drop cloths, etc.)	50
Total Start-up Expenses	$230
B. Other fixed expenses	none
Total fixed costs	230

Variable costs

Tim's customers will provide ladders. He will provide the paint. His neighborhood has tract homes, all approximately the same size. A local paint supplier has agreed to sell Tim his high-quality paint at a twenty percent discount, for $6 per gallon. He estimates it will take about ten gallons per house.

Costs per customer:

Paint	$60
Brushes	8
Turpentine/cleaner	2
Rags	2
Total variable costs per customer	$72

Fourth: Establish your price

Method One:

Tim calls around to get quotes from the competition. He gets three quotes for a typical size house in his neighborhood:

Jones Paint Service	$500
Pete's Painting	$550
Quality Painting	$450

Therefore, the average professional painter charges $500, which includes all paint and supplies. Using this method, and discounting thirty percent for Tim's inexperience, he decides to charge:

Average professional price	$500
Less 30% ($500 × .30)	(150)
Tim's price	$350

Method Two:

Step 1. Tim wants to earn at least $6 per hour.

Step 2. After painting his own house, he estimates it will take him an average of forty hours per house, which includes buying the paint and supplies, preparation work and painting.

Step 3. His variable costs are $72 per house.

Step 4.

Time estimate:		hours per customer
× Wages	$ 6	per hour
= Total wages	$240	
Plus add in:	$ 72	**Variable costs**
Equals:	$312	**Final price**

Both price methods end up with similar prices: $350 versus $312. Tim will have some *fixed* start-up costs, so he decides to use the $350 price, which will still put him well below his competition but will ensure he makes his $6 per hour goal.

Fifth: Estimate how much business you expect.
By the end of April, Tim already has three of his neighbors lined up for summer painting. He can only handle one customer per week, four customers per month. Tim feels he can easily fill up this schedule by distributing advertising flyers door to door during April. So, his income estimates are:

June	4 customers × $350	$1400
July	4 customers × $350	$1400
August	4 customers × $350	$1400
Total income		$4200

The next page includes Tim's business plan worksheet for you to use as an example. Notice that it includes space for calculating total costs, and for subtracting costs from income to arrive at an estimated profit (or loss).

Your Business Plan

Immediately following Tim's example plan is a blank worksheet for your use in preparing a business plan. Follow through all five steps, filling in the blanks on the worksheet with the information you have already prepared on the preceding pages.

One Year Business Plan for:
Tim's Housepainting Service

Month:

Income:	1 JAN	2 FEB	3 MAR	4 APR	5 MAY	6 JUN	7 JUL	8 AUG	9 SEP	10 OCT	11 NOV	12 DEC	Total
# of Customers/Products						4	4	4					12
× Price = Income						1400	1400	1400					$4200
+ Miscellaneous Income						–	–	–					
Total Income						1400	1400	1400					$4200

Costs:	JAN	FEB	MAR	APR	MAY	JUN	JUL	AUG	SEP	OCT	NOV	DEC	Total
Fixed: Startup				20[1]	210[2]	–	–	–					$ 230
Other													
Variable: (# Customers × Cost)						288	288	288					$ 864
Total Costs				20	210	288	288	288					$1094

	JAN	FEB	MAR	APR	MAY	JUN	JUL	AUG	SEP	OCT	NOV	DEC	Total
Profit/(loss)*				(20)	(210)	1112	1112	1112					$3106

*Profit/(loss) = Total Income − Total Costs
[1]Advertising flyers
[2]Paint sprayer & miscellaneous

One Year Business Plan for:

_____

Month:	1	2	3	4	5	6	7	8	9	10	11	12	
Income:	JAN	FEB	MAR	APR	MAY	JUN	JUL	AUG	SEP	OCT	NOV	DEC	**Total**
# of Cus-tomers/ Products													
× Price = Income													
+ Miscel-laneous Income													
Total Income													

Costs:													**Total**
Fixed: Startup													
Other													
Variable: (# Customers × Cost)													
Total Costs													

													Total
Profit/ (loss)*													

*Profit/(loss) = Total Income − Total Costs

Step 4 Register with the Government

There are four levels of government you need to consider:

Federal   State   County   City

The Federal Government

▶ **Social Security Number** Before you begin ANY kind of work, either for yourself or for wages, you must first obtain a social security number through the Social Security Administration of the U.S. Department of Health and Human Services. If you are under eighteen years old, you may apply for a number by mail; otherwise, go to a branch office for an interview. Look in your phone book for the number and location of the office nearest you. If there is no office in your town or county, call long distance directory assistance for your area (1-YOUR AREA CODE-555-1212). They'll be able to give you a phone number to call. To apply for a social security number, you'll need to have an original or certified copy of your birth certificate, plus one other form of verifiable ID, such as a baptismal record. Your local office can tell you what kinds of ID are acceptable. It normally takes about four weeks to receive your social security number.

▶ **Employer Identification Number** (only if you have employees) If you will be operating as a sole proprietorship, *you don't need to register with the U.S. government* to begin operation. The only exception to this is if you will be hiring employees. Then, you would need to apply for an Employer Identification Number. The author strongly advises you *not* to hire employees. But if you feel you must, contact the Internal Revenue Service for form SS-4, Application for Employer Identification Number. Their toll-free number to order tax forms is 1-800-424-3676.

State Government

Laws and regulations governing small businesses vary from state to state. Check with your local Small Business Administration, Chamber of Commerce or state officials if you have any questions about registration requirements.

▶ **Sales Tax Permit** You don't need to register a small business with the state unless you will be selling products or services directly to the public that are subject to state sales tax. Sometimes, service businesses are exempt from state tax. Check with your state tax office for more information. Some of the ventures described in this book do involve "retail" sales, that is, selling products directly to consumers. In most states, you WILL need a sales tax permit for businesses such as Idea #28, T-shirts, or any of the mail-order products. If you will be selling items to a store representing your products, then you do NOT need a sales tax permit. The store will be selling your products to consumers and will collect sales tax right at the store. If you'll be selling products to stores for resale, some states require you to apply for a Wholesale Exemption Certificate, which excuses you from paying sales tax. Check with your state authorities.

▶ **Unemployment Tax Number** (only if you have employees) The only other state requirement you may have to meet is determined by whether you have employees. If so, you must apply for a state unemployment compensation tax number. Check with the local office of your State Unemployment Commission for the form.

County government
Usually, you'll need to file a simple form at your county courthouse, probably at the county clerk's office. The purpose of county registration is simply to register the name of your business, to make sure no one else is operating with the same business name within the county. Normally, a small fee, usually under $5, accompanies your registration. Each county's requirements are different. Check with your county clerk.

City government
Typically, you won't need to register with your city to operate a small business out of your home.

▶ **Zoning ordinances** Most cities don't require a permit or license, but they do have certain zoning ordinances governing small business operations within city limits. Some cities have extremely strict rules. For example, many cities specifically forbid small business owners working out of their homes to have employees working there. Some prohibit seeing customers in a residence. However, there aren't many cases where cities have actually prosecuted "illegal" activities such as Tupperware parties or piano lessons given in a private home. Also, many zoning ordinances forbid storage of business equipment or supplies in bulky storage buildings on your lawn. Check with your city about local regulations; start with your department of planning and zoning.

▶ **City Sales Tax** Few major metropolitan areas assess a city sales tax. If yours does, you'll have to fill out an application for a tax permit similar to the state form—*but only if your business sells retail goods directly to consumers.* Your city clerk should be able to tell you if your city collects a city sales tax and provide you with the necessary form.

This section on government registration covers only requirements for *starting up* a business. You will have to prepare other government documents to pay taxes or keep track of employees if you hire help. These are covered in Chapter 7.

Child Labor Laws

As a self-employed entrepreneur, you are exempt from the Child Labor Laws. However, if you employ anyone under the age of eighteen, you'll need to understand the important provisions of the 1983 Fair Labor Standards Act. This act is intended to protect kids from work that could interfere with their health or well-being. NOTE: Some states have recently passed legislation governing teenagers and work hours that are even stricter than the federal Child Labor Laws. Check with your State Department of Labor to see if any of their laws cover you. Below is a summary of the provisions of the FEDERAL law relevant to you only if you are an EMPLOYER of people under age eighteen:

1. Minors age eighteen and over may be engaged in ANY occupation, for an unlimited amount of hours.

2. Minors age sixteen and seventeen may work in any occupation the Department of Labor declares is nonhazardous, for unlimited hours. The Department of Labor lists seventeen "hazardous" occupations, none of which are included in this book as business ventures. Some of them are:

Coal mining	Slaughtering or meatpacking
Logging and sawmilling	
Any exposure to radioactive substances	Roofing operations

3. Teenagers age fourteen and fifteen may work outside of school hours in NONmanufacturing, NONmining, NONhazardous jobs. They may work no more than three hours on a school day, eighteen hours in a school week, eight hours on a nonschool day or forty hours in a nonschool week. They may not begin work before 7 a.m. or work after

7 p.m., except from June 1 through Labor Day. Then evening hours are extended to 9 p.m. NOTE: Minors under age sixteen may not perform work that requires climbing ladders or the use of scaffolding.

4. The government doesn't allow kids age twelve and thirteen to work, unless it is

▶ On a farm with their parents' consent

▶ In their parents' business, unless hazardous

▶ Delivering newspapers

▶ Working in movies, TV or radio

▶ Working in the home making wreaths

If you want additional information on how the child labor laws affect you, contact your local Department of Labor office. They can answer questions by phone or send you one of their pamphlets.

To summarize, your obligations to all levels of government *before* you begin business are:

Federal government

1. Obtain a social security number.
2. Apply for an employer identification number ONLY if you will be hiring employees.
3. Check the Child Labor Laws only if you plan to hire employees under age eighteen.

State government

1. Apply for a state sales tax permit ONLY if you are selling retail products or services directly to the public that are subject to taxation.
2. Apply for an unemployment compensation tax number ONLY if you will be hiring employees.

County government

1. Register your business name with the county clerk.

City government

1. Check with the planning and zoning commission to see if your business complies with local ordinances.

2. Apply for a city sales tax permit ONLY if you are selling retail products directly to the public AND if you live in one of the few large cities that have their own sales tax.

Federal laws regulating small businesses are few and straightforward. However, small business regulations vary widely from state to state, county and city, so it's always wise to contact the local authorities before you begin.

Step 5 Set Up a Recordkeeping System
Before you begin business, you will need to set up a simple bookkeeping system to keep track of your costs and revenue. This is described in detail in Chapter 6.

Step 6 Set Up a Bank Account
It is NOT necessary for you to set up a business bank account, but it IS highly recommended. The advantages of having a separate account for your business are:

▶ It demonstrates to the Internal Revenue Service that you are a serious business operator.

▶ It provides backup records, besides just your bookkeeping system, of your expenses and revenue. You might need this in the outside chance you are audited by the Internal Revenue Service.

▶ It's good experience learning the ropes of banking.

▶ It provides you with a credit reference which can be used in the future to help you qualify for a loan.

The only disadvantage of keeping a separate bank account for your business is that sometimes the fees are high. Fees vary from bank to bank, and depending on the type of account you set up. Shop around for the best rates. Most bankers are quite willing to sit down with you to explain their various fees and services in detail.

Step 7 Raise Money
Step 7 isn't necessary for most of the business ideas in this book. However, some of them will require money to set up. Here are some ideas to minimize the cash you'll need in the beginning:

▶ **Try to get by with what you have.** Don't think you need to run out and buy $7,000 worth of computer equipment for Idea #41, Personalized Greeting Cards. Use a computer you already have access to, or forget it.

▶ **Hold down your expenses in the beginning.** Try to get by with minimal equipment and supplies at first, paying for what you need later out of income you earn from the business. For example, for Idea #1, Auto Detailing, you don't need fancy equipment, such as an electric auto polisher, to begin your business. Wait and see if the business takes off first. Then, if you have an avalanche of orders, you'll have plenty of money to buy equipment later.

▶ **Beg and borrow everything you possibly can.** Take advantage of every free resource you can get your hands on. Borrow a parent's copy machine, use the school typewriter, borrow art supplies for advertising from friends. Ask for donations of used office supplies. Don't underestimate your ability to get something for nothing. Usually, adults are happy to lend equipment or supplies to enterprising youth.

▶ **Don't overdo it in the beginning!** There's a great temptation to buy loads of shiny new equipment, office supplies, files, etc. when starting a business. *Anyone* can impress customers with fancy business doodads. It's your challenge to impress them with *you* and your own abilities, without the fancy gimmicks. Get by on a shoestring. The shrewd manager pays just as close attention to cutting costs as to boosting income.

▶ **Try to find good used materials first.** In most cases, used supplies and equipment can serve the purpose just as well as new, for a fraction of the price. Used file cabinets, typewriters, computers, desks, lawn equipment, and vehicles are just a few of the things you can get great deals on. Check out a local salvage store, the Goodwill store or the want ads in your local newspaper.

We've covered the bases about how *not* to spend money in the beginning. If you still think you need some front-end operating cash (necessary only for a few of the Fifty Ideas), try these methods:

▶ After you have perfected your business plan, take it to a family member or other adult you are close to. People who care about you will probably lend you money if they can afford to—and if your plan shows you'll be able to pay them back within a reasonable amount of time. If you *do* set up a loan with friends or family, write up a brief, informal IOU document.

State the terms of the loan: total amount, payment plan, interest rate, and date of final payment. Both parties need to sign and date it. Then, *stick to it.*

▶ Check around your room. Normally, everyone has extra stuff lying around they can part with to get extra cash. How about that bike you don't use? Or an old chemistry set? Books? Sports equipment? Ask your family for used items that you can sell to raise cash. You can get money for your old things by having a garage sale, by advertising in the newspapers or by posting ads in public places like the grocery store. Some larger cities have salvage stores that will pay you a (very) modest amount for used items.

▶ Ask permission to use your parents' credit card. If you can convince them you are serious about your new venture, and will earn enough money to pay your portion of the bill when it comes, they may be willing to do this. If you can't pay the entire bill off the first month, be sure to cover *your* portion of the interest charges. *Don't* fall into the trap of easy money. If you use this approach, be very careful what you spend and don't go overboard.

▶ Consider taking in one or more partners who have cash available. Before you do, you should also consider the problems associated with a partnership. It complicates your accounting and tax preparation. You must have a written partnership agreement spelling out who does what in the relationship, which usually requires the services of a business attorney. Plus, the relationship can be difficult to manage. One partner can end up doing the lion's share of the work. Business relationships can really strain a friendship. You *can* draw up an agreement that gives a partner a small percentage of the profits simply for kicking in some cash, where you do all the work and make all the decisions. However, this arrangement might be difficult to sell before you actually start earning money. Consider a partnership arrangement only if you can't raise cash any other way. Then, select your partner(s) wisely. Be sure you can work well with them, and that they will pitch in and do their share of the work.

▶ If you have tried all the methods above and still can't raise any cash, simply pick another venture out of this book that doesn't need a front-end investment.

One word of caution: don't expect to be able to raise cash from the usual sources that adults use. Bankers, financial institutions and venture capitalists won't touch teenage businesses, unless you have substantial stocks, bonds, savings or other valuable assets in your *own* name. In that case, you probably don't need a loan anyway.

So much for the step-by-step approach to starting up a business. That wasn't too bad, was it? Now, *good luck* on your new venture, and begin with STEP 1: FIRST, READ THE REST OF THIS BOOK!

4

Fifty Business
Ventures

The following pages contain fifty ideas for teenage business ventures, plus a section on special ideas for earning money around the holidays. The fifty ideas are intended to be run as professional business ventures, using the step-by-step approach outlined in Chapter 3. (If you haven't read Chapter 3 yet, be sure you do before you set up shop.) There are outdoor and indoor neighborhood services, school-based ventures, services that utilize special skills, ways to make money with a personal computer, and transportation and mail-order ventures. See what appeals to you. Then check your selection against the guidelines in Chapter 3.

Neighborhood Ventures—
Outside Work

1. Auto Detailing
2. Garage Sale Service
3. Recycling
4. Neighborhood Directory
5. House Numbers
6. Painting Fences
7. Painting Houses
8. Pool Service
9. Home Improvement— Safety and Energy Efficiency
10. Shrub Maintenance
11. Garage Cleaning
12. Lawn Service

The twelve ideas in this section all involve out-of-doors work. If you live in a cold climate, some of the business ventures will be limited to warmer months. However, Ideas 3, 4,

9 and 11 can provide steady, year-round income no matter what the climate.

Idea

Auto Detailing

Job Description: Custom car care

Personal Traits Required: Careful attention to detail

Experience Required: Practice washing cars

Materials Required: Car wash detergent, sponge, bucket, chamois, vinyl cleaner, high suction vacuum cleaner & extension cord, glass cleaner, rags

Supplemental Materials: Chrome cleaner, tire cleaner, rubbing compound, windshield wiper fluid, brake fluid, transmission fluid, oil, oil pan, tire pump, car wax, rug shampoo, power buffer, battery tester, coolant tester, antifreeze/coolant

Marketing Method: Door-to-door flyer

Expected Wages: $5 to $10 per hour

At present, if car owners want to get their autos clean, they have only four basic options:

1. Do it themselves
2. Run it through the automatic car wash
3. Use one of the high-pressure hose car washes
4. Go to a professional "executive" car care company—they usually wash, wax and clean cars by hand

There are drawbacks to all four, which means there's an opportunity for you to make money by offering a fifth type of service. Many people don't have time for Option 1, or don't do a very good job. Automatic car washes are inadequate for thorough exterior cleaning, and don't do anything for the inside of the car. Option 3, the high-pressure hose car wash, doesn't do much more than Option 2; the owner still must finish the interior work. Option 4, the executive car care or auto detailer, is becoming more popular. In many cities, demand is booming for individualized, professional car cleaning. The auto detailer or "executive car care" company offers a total package of cleaning services, from inside out. The drawback to this for the average car owner is price. The going rate for auto detailing at a professional shop is $30 for a basic wash to $185, which includes waxing and buffing. A good auto detailer provides some or all of these services to their customers:

▶ Hand washing exterior

▶ Vacuuming interior

▶ Vacuuming trunk

▶ Shampooing interior carpets and upholstery

▶ Cleaning and dressing interior vinyl or leather surfaces

▶ Finish spot removal

▶ Cleaning and dressing vinyl tops

▶ Cleaning glass and mirrors

▶ Removing and cleaning floor mats

▶ Cleaning tires

▶ Cleaning and polishing chrome surfaces

▶ Waxing and buffing exterior

Depending upon your skills, you should be able to offer some or all of these as a service to your neighbors. If you offered just a basic interior and exterior car cleaning at your customers' homes, it could include:

▶ Hand washing exterior

▶ Wiping down interior vinyl or leather surfaces

▶ Vacuuming interior

▶ Cleaning glass surfaces

You should be able to price this at $20 and up, depending on what you offer. It would depend upon your speed and ability. Your neighbors won't be willing to pay you unless you can demonstrate a superior quality of service, better than they would do themselves. Practice on your family car(s) or friends' vehicles until you know exactly how long it should take to do a good job. Check your finished work thoroughly! Look for streaks on the exterior finish and glass, or any dirty spots you might have missed. Get someone else in your family to critique your work and provide suggestions. Remember, customers are picky about paying for a luxury service. If you can't offer high quality, they will do it themselves in the future—or pay one of your competitors. To avoid disaster, use your own products rather than trust whatever your customers may have in their garage.

Make your service special by providing some simple preventive maintenance for your customers. If you do offer these additional services, you could probably bump your price well above the $20 range. Try including checking some or all of the following as part of your service:

▶ tire pressure

▶ brake fluid

▶ transmission fluid

▶ antifreeze/coolant

▶ oil

▶ windshield wiper solution

▶ battery charge

You could give the customer a checklist of these items, marking those that need service or replacement. If you have the expertise, you could add fluids or pump up tires, but you will need to charge extra for supplies. These are simple things you could do which don't take much time, but will boost your income and help you sell your service.

If you can do a competent job at waxing and chrome and tire cleaning, offer a more complete package for a higher price. Considering the high price and the labor involved, you could probably charge at least $30 for such a service. (Professionals in big cities charge up to $185 for complete car detailing, but they usually include engine steam cleaning, a service you will not be able to provide.) The important thing is timing. Check to see how long it takes you to do a thorough job, and price the service so that it earns you at least $5 per hour. That will still make your service cost far less than the car care companies.

The most effective way to advertise will probably be a door-to-door flyer. Your strongest selling points are your low price and your convenience—you can come to their door. If your prices are super low, compare your rates to the competition right in the ad. Be specific about what services you include. Stress quality, perhaps even guaranteeing satisfaction or money back. Have some references ready when prospective customers call. When selling your service, try to sign your customers up for a regular cleaning schedule. Building a good business requires repeat customers. Don't forget, this is a service that would make an ideal gift for a special occasion, like Father's Day. Sell coupons for a future car wash for customers to stick in birthday or other special occasion cards.

Another marketing strategy might be to offer your service to a local auto repair or body shop that doesn't presently offer detailing services. For the use of one of their indoor bays, you could be available certain hours per week to detail their customers' cars. Offer the garage owner a percentage of your profits, say 25 percent. That way, you could provide your service year-round, regardless of the local weather or climate. Plus, the local garage will help to plug your service. If you can arrange such a deal, prepare a large poster advertising your detailing service and hours, and hang it in a prominent location in the owner's shop.

Idea
2

Garage Sale Service

Job Description: Resale store owner/manager

Personal Traits Required: Strong organizational skills, ability to keep good records

Experience Required: None, but some bookkeeping would be helpful

Materials Required: A large open space you can use on a regular basis, such as a garage or empty corner of a parking lot, plus hanging racks and display tables. A pickup truck would come in handy but is not essential.

Marketing Method: Signs in the neighborhood, door-to-door flyer, newspaper ads.

Expected Wages: Unlimited potential

Most people have good, used items around the house that they want to get rid of, and everybody would like to get some money for such "junk." However, it's a real bother trying to sell one or two items. Many families would like to hold a garage sale, but a really successful garage sale needs a large quantity of goods for sale. People rarely stop at a garage sale that offers only a handful of beat-up items. That's where YOU can come in.

Almost every neighborhood could benefit from a regularly scheduled, well-organized garage sale. If you can arrange to have a garage or other large space on a regular basis, then this idea is perfect for you.

First, determine a schedule for your sales. A one-shot sale doesn't have much income potential. Holding a permanent garage sale every day will waste a lot of your time. Families don't shop garage sales except on weekends. So, scheduling a sale every Saturday or two Saturdays a month would be about right.

Next, determine your sale policies. These policies are completely up to you, but the following should give you some guidelines:

1. Pricing Garage sale shoppers come looking for *bargains!* Used items should be priced at 50% of their retail value if they are in almost perfect condition, and far less if they appear well-used. You should let your customers price their own merchandise, within reason. Caution them if the price appears too high. You won't be able to sell a used record album for $7, for example.

2. Your fee There are two approaches to charging your customers.

▶ Setting a flat fee for each item, like $2 each, or

▶ Charging a percentage of the sales price.

The fee you charge must cover your time during the sale, plus all the time you spend marketing and organizing the sale, plus expenses of advertising and supplies. You could set a sliding scale of fees, depending on the value of the merchandise. The percentage should be higher for small items, and less for expensive items. For example, you could charge 20% of the price of all goods under $50, and 10% for all goods over $50. Thus, your fee on a $1 kitchen spoon would be 20 cents, and your fee on a $100 sofa would be $10. Remember, the market for used goods isn't great. You are offering a service to your customers. If you didn't sell it for them, they probably would end up giving it away to charity. Getting 80% for used goods is better than nothing!

3. Merchandise You'll need to set some rules about the merchandise you accept. Take only merchandise in reasonably good condition. No one will buy a sofa with the springs hanging out, no matter how low the price. Also, you might want a rule that electrical appliances must be in working condition. Buyers won't want a radio that doesn't play, because they won't know how much it will cost to fix. Clothes should be washed and in good repair, with rips mended and buttons firmly affixed.

4. Delivery and pickup You can ask your customers to deliver the goods at a set time, say Friday night after 5:00 p.m. for a

Saturday sale. Then, set a time for them to come after the sale to pick up their money and any unsold items. Be firm about the pickup time. You don't want other people's junk in your family garage all week. You might state that all items not picked up by a specified time will be donated to charity. Then make arrangements for the charity to come and take away the leftovers. If you have a pickup truck, you may want to offer pickup and delivery service. If you do, charge a flat fee, say $10.

5. Marking the merchandise Customers should be responsible for marking their own items. The price and their name should be clearly visible on every item for sale. If it will make it easier for you, hand out some standard tags for marking. Color coding tags may also make your recordkeeping easier.

6. Recordkeeping Prepare a standard recordkeeping form to give each customer. The example below is for Dave's Garage Sale Service. Dave has decided to set his fees at twenty percent for items less than $100, and ten percent for items over $100.

Before the sale, customers should itemize *everything* they give you on a form similar to the example. Each item listed should contain a brief description and the price. Then, go over this list together, checking prices and quantities as you take delivery of the goods. Each of you should sign and date the form. This will keep you out of serious trouble that might arise if the customer accuses you of theft or mismarking a price. Keep all the forms handy at the sale, filing them alphabetically by name. Then, as buyers purchase items, check for the customer's name on the sales tag. Pull the customer's form and check off each item as it's sold. When customers come to get their unsold goods and money, take out their records. In the customer's presence, total up the amount received, subtracting your fee and paying your customer the rest.

Example
Dave's Garage Sale Service

Description	Qty	Price Each	Total Price	Qty Sold	Total Due
Items less than $100:					
Men's dress shirts	10	$ 3	$ 30	7	$ 21
Assorted baby clothes	15	2	30	9	18
Subtotal	25		$ 60	16	$ 39
Items over $100					
Sofa	1	100	100	1	100
Total	26		$160	17	$139

Amount due customer:

Items less than $100: $39 × 80% = $ 31

Items over $100: $100 × 90% = ___90

Total due customer: $121

Signed: _____ Date: _____
Customer

_____ Date: _____
(Your signature)

7. Payment You should probably ask for payment from the buyers *strictly in cash*. That really simplifies matters, and makes it easier to pay your customers at the end of the sale.

8. Sale pricing Many garage sale shoppers want to haggle over prices and drive the prices down. If you "bargain" over every item, you will shortly lose your mind! It will take too much of your valuable time, and the recordkeeping will turn into a nightmare. If you accept less for an item than the marked price, your customers could then easily accuse you of shorting them cash. You could lose their trust and repeat business. Avoid problems by posting a sign which clearly states, "ALL PRICES FIRM."

The best way to find merchandise for sale will be the door-to-door flyer. State all of your policies in the flyer. Also, list the schedule and location of the sale.

The hardest part of this business will be to find buyers. There's so much competition. Work at being the biggest and the best! Post notices everywhere, and signs in the neighborhood with your address to call attention to the sale. Use newspaper advertising if local signs don't generate enough buyers. The advantage of a regular garage sale is that you *will* get a lot of repeat buyers. Stress the size of your garage sale—THE ENTIRE NEIGHBORHOOD OF HOOTERVILLE GARAGE SALE—for example.

Idea

Recycling

Job Description: Door-to-door pickup of recyclable goods

Personal Traits Required: Good organizational skills

Experience Required: None

Materials Required: You can get by with large trash bags and a hand-drawn wagon. A bicycle, moped or car would be helpful, but not necessary.

Marketing Method: Door-to-door flyer

Expected Wages: Unlimited potential

Most people would like to do their civic duty and recycle their newspapers, cans, glass bottles or grocery bags. The fact is, they rarely do. It's too much of a hassle, so they simply pitch recyclables with the rest of their trash. This is a waste of valuable resources *and* money. You can turn the situation to your advantage.

Offer a neighborhood recycling service by scheduling regular pickups of recyclable goods. The key to success in this business is to make it as *simple* as possible for your customers, and to provide extremely reliable service.

First, check with local sources to find out where you can deliver recyclable goods for payment in CASH. Most large towns have a location for recycling aluminum cans. It's harder to find places to return glass containers or newspapers. You might want to call a manufacturer or newspaper company directly for information on recycling.

If you determine that you can get money for recycling, then you're in business. First, set up a schedule for your route. You might want to do different blocks on different days. Then, circulate a flyer door to door, advertising your service. Explain *what* you want to recycle, and *when* you will pick it up. You cannot offer to pay your customers for their items; otherwise, there won't be enough money left over for you. Your customers should be willing to donate these items to you as a convenience for themselves and as their civic duty. Stress the importance of recycling right in your advertising. "Save a tree, donate your newspapers to Jim's Recycling Service," for example. They'll be more willing to donate if you state in your ad that you will be using the money for a worthwhile cause, such as your college fund.

When customers contact you for service, arrange with them to leave the items outside their home in a convenient spot, so they don't have to be home for the pickup. Set a day of the week and approximate time for the pickup. Keep all this information in a customer notebook.

One word of caution. Some states, such as Michigan, have large deposits on some recyclable goods, such as aluminum cans. It will be difficult, if not impossible, to get people to donate items they can get money for at their local grocery stores.

Idea

4

Neighborhood Directory

Job Description: Publisher of a neighborhood reference booklet

Personal Traits Required: Strong organizational skills and outgoing personality

Experience Required: Some typing ability

Materials Required: Access to a typewriter or word processor, paper, and a printer or copy machine

Marketing Method: Door-to-door flyer AND canvassing

Expected Wages: Unlimited potential

Almost everybody would like to know more about their neighborhood and the people in it. You can provide a very useful service to your neighbors and make money in the process by putting together a neighborhood directory. This can be a simple listing of people's names and addresses, or you can be quite ambitious. Make it really snazzy by including quality reference material about the neighborhood and community, such as information about local parks, churches, day care, schools, community events, emergency phone numbers (fire, police, poison control), etc. If you want to be really ambitious, you could also sell advertising space in the directory to local merchants.

The place to start is with the door-to-door flyer. Briefly describe your directory and what it provides. Include a form to fill out that they can tear off and return to you, with the information you need. Indicate whether you will pick up the completed forms, or include a self-addressed, stamped envelope for return to you. You might want to ask them for:

- ▶ Names of adults
- ▶ Names and ages of children
- ▶ Occupation of husband and wife
- ▶ Address and phone number

If you go beyond this basic information, people might object that you are snooping into their personal affairs. In your ad, state that you will be selling the directories, the price, and the date they will be available. Include a statement that there is no obligation to BUY a directory—everyone will be included, regardless of whether or not they buy one. Put a requested return date for the information. After that date, assemble all your returned forms. Then, go door to door to collect all the missing households.

After you have collected your data, assemble it into a useful format. The best way to list names for a neighborhood directory is in STREET NUMBER ORDER, with a cross-reference index in the back of names listed alphabetically with their corresponding street address. Type up the list, using a typewriter or word processor.

Once the list is prepared, then use it to sell advertising. Don't attempt to sell ads until your list is substantially complete. Merchants will have a hard time believing in your directory until you have something real to show them. Check with the local newspaper for display advertising rates (see information on display advertising in Chapter 5), then price your ads at a fraction of that cost. As you visit local merchants, do a double sales job. Don't just sell advertising—sell them the directories as well. Explain how useful a neighborhood directory would be to them, particularly for such occupations as insurance sales, financial brokers, or realtors.

When you have assembled all the material, the names, the ads, and perhaps some local community information, then bind it with a durable cover. Be sure to include the name of your neighborhood and the selling price right on the cover. You could prepare some artwork and print it on colorful card stock, or simply use a three-ring punch and put it in an inexpensive plastic cover.

When you are ready to sell the directories, first go door to door. Leave a message about the directory and your phone number at the houses with no one home. Then, canvass local businesses, schools, and institutions. They may wish to buy the booklets in quantities. Try to sell quantities to real estate agents who are helping families move into your neighborhood. Also, you could arrange to sell quantities to a local bookstore, grocery or drug store. If you sell to merchants for resale, you will have to give a discount off the cover price so they can make money, too. Say your cover price is $2.50. Offer to sell copies at $1.75 each if a merchant takes a minimum order of fifty, for example.

Don't treat this as a one-time only business. If you have a very small town, include the entire community and update the book annually. The book should sell all year long, particularly if you market it actively at school and to businesses. If you live in a larger town, keep the book restricted to a well-defined neighborhood. Then, after you finish one neighborhood's booklet, start on another. Another money-making idea is to produce directories for community service organizations, clubs, or professional groups. It might be easier to sell to these professional groups if you can show them a neighborhood directory you have already prepared.

Idea
5

House Numbers

Job Description: Painter of house numbers on curbs or sidewalks

Personal Traits Required: Neatness

Experience Required: None

Materials Required: Paint & brushes, cardboard number stencils

Supplemental Materials: Plastic stick-on, brass, wood, or cast-iron house numbers

Marketing Method: Door-to-door flyer or canvassing

Expected Wages: At least $5 per hour

There's nothing more irritating than trying to locate a house in a neighborhood where the house numbers aren't clearly marked. Most neighborhoods don't have uniform house number markings. It's usually up to homeowners to post the number on their homes, mailboxes or curbs.

You can provide an inexpensive house number service by going door to door and painting numbers on curbs. Neat and uniform house numbering is not only a convenience to visitors and mail carriers, it is an important safety precaution so that emergency vehicles can locate an address in a hurry.

The only materials needed are paint, brushes and stencils so that each number can be drawn neatly. Spend the extra money to buy good quality paint. It's hard to find, but you can buy special paint that reflects in the dark which would be an added selling feature. Be sure to *practice* painting before you try it on customers.

This is a business usually done by students, and the going rate is anywhere from $4 to $10. The actual number painting shouldn't take you more than twenty minutes. It does take some advance planning, though. The best way to organize this business is to pass out flyers door to door a few days prior to the day you want to paint. Explain your service and its benefits. The bottom half of the flyer should be a permission slip with the customer's name, address, telephone number, order information and place for signature. Ask customers to post their flyers in an envelope on their front door. Remind them to include their signature for permission, plus a check for payment. Customers will be more apt to trust you if you explain you are a neighbor and list your address and telephone number right in the ad.

Door-to-door canvassing isn't as effective these days for two reasons: many people aren't home during the day, and those who are have become reluctant to answer the door for safety reasons. However, you might want to follow up at houses that didn't post permission on their doors, just to double-check they really don't want the service.

Boost sales by offering a package deal that includes a house number in the front and rear for customers who have an alley. Also, you can expand by offering a total house number service. You could also sell inexpensive plastic stick-on numbers and letters for mailboxes, charging by the letter or digit. Or you could locate a supplier of high-quality brass, cast-iron or wooden numbers that you can affix right to the front of the house.

Idea

6

Painting Fences

Job Description: Custom fence painting

Personal Traits Required: Patience and careful attention to detail

Experience Required: Prior painting experience is helpful, but not required

Materials Required: Paint or stain, brushes or paint sprayer

Marketing Method: Door-to-door flyer

Expected Wages: $5 per hour

Painting fences is hard work, but can be financially rewarding. It's difficult to find someone willing to paint fences, and most people are put off by the astronomical fees charged by professional painters. If your neighborhood is filled with unpainted fences, you could develop a very profitable business.

Practice painting some fences first, to determine how long it takes you. You should be able to develop reliable time estimates through practice. Application of paint or stain by brush is extremely slow. If you can, invest in a paint sprayer. New electric sprayers can be bought for around $100. If you use a sprayer, you must be very careful not to get paint on surrounding objects. You can hold up a large piece of cardboard behind the area you're spraying to cut down on paint splatter. Follow the sprayer directions exactly, because some paints can't be applied through a sprayer. Sprayers have two disadvantages:

1.   They typically use 20 to 30% more paint than brush application, and

2.   You *cannot* use a sprayer if the wind is blowing much harder than a gentle breeze.

Because of your age, you must attract business by providing really cheap service, compared to professionals. One way to offer a price advantage is to locate a paint supplier who will give you a discount, rather than having your customer buy the paint himself. When you make a customer call, have samples of your paint or stain colors with you for convenient selection. When setting a price, charge enough to cover the paint plus paying yourself a wage of at least $5 per hour. This should keep your price significantly lower than the pros. (Caution: you won't be able to earn reliable profits until you can make accurate estimates of how much paint you need and how long it will take you to paint.) Call a few painters in your area to compare your price, making sure your price is reasonable. If you will be providing paint, ask for 50% payment before you begin so you can purchase the paint; then, 50% is due upon completion.

Spend some time discussing proper painting techniques and the type of paint or stain that's appropriate for your area with your local paint store expert. Wood fences eat up a lot of paint, usually more than the recommendation on paint can labels. A local expert can provide you with more reliable estimates of paint needs. Your paint supplier will be more than happy to help, and will probably have brochures you can read and study.

Advertise your service with door-to-door flyers and signs posted in your neighborhood. If you have reliable transportation, advertise in the newspaper to reach a wider audience. Emphasize your low price and guarantee your service in the ads. Because every fence is different, you can't state your price in the ad; however, offer free estimates. State that fence painting or staining actually saves money by extending the life of the fence.

Many painters have small aluminum signs printed, with their name and telephone number, that they hang as a permanent advertisement on their completed work. That way, people who drive by can see your work long after you have finished. Contact a local sign company to check prices.

Keep the paint on the fence, and not on your customers' houses or prize rose bushes. You *must* be neat, cleaning up thoroughly after you're finished. No matter how low the price, you'll end up with angry customers and a shoddy reputation if you don't clean up properly. When you finish a job, make sure your customers are satisfied. If they aren't, fix the problem. If they are, ask permission to use them as references. The key to this business is customer satisfaction and good references.

Idea

7

Painting Houses

Job Description: Exterior house painter

Personal Traits Required: You must be neat, thorough and pay careful attention to small details. Upper body strength is needed to paint for long stretches at a time.

Experience Required: You MUST have experience painting at least a house or two before you can do an adequate job.

Materials Required: Paintbrushes, rollers, rags, paint thinner. Paint and ladders can be supplied by you or your customer. A power paint sprayer is handy but not absolutely required.

Marketing Method: Door-do-door flyer

Expected Wages: At least $5 per hour

The one big area where teens have a real opportunity is in the service business dominated by expensive professionals, but where teens can do an adequate job for far less. House painting is one of those outstanding opportunities. Don't attempt to paint houses unless you have some experience. It does take skill and careful attention to detail to do a good job. You must have patience to do an adequate job of surface preparation and then to paint neatly around windows, doors, eaves and architectural detail. If you want to paint but have no experience, try ideas #5 or #6 before attempting to paint houses.

Before you launch into this venture, go to your library or home improvement center and pick up a book on house painting. You need to understand all the work involved. It isn't just slapping paint on with a brush. You can pick up tips at a local paint or lumber store. Some of the giant warehouse-type lumber stores offer free seminars on house painting techniques.

You can pick up experience by offering to paint a neighbor's house at bargain-basement rates. Keep track of how long it takes, and practice the techniques you have read about. In order to earn good money, you'll need to be able to make accurate estimates of how long each house will take. For example, an older, wooden frame house takes as long to prepare for painting (scraping, sanding, etc.) as actually putting on the paint. This isn't obvious until you practice!

If homes in your neighborhood are fairly standard, you could offer fixed prices based upon size, number of stories and windows. Otherwise, you will have to estimate every job before quoting a price. Offer free estimates. After you have determined how long it takes you to paint a house, get a few quotes from professionals on what *they* would charge for a similar job. Your price needs to be well below that. You'll need to decide if you will provide paint and ladders, or have your customers provide them. If you have transportation, include paint and ladders as part of your service. Just as in the fence painting idea, if you plan to include paint, find a store that will give you a discount on your supplies.

If you can afford it, purchase a power paint sprayer suitable for heavy-duty use on exteriors. It will cut your painting time to a fraction of brush application. Brushes will still be needed for trim work.

If you don't have transportation, advertise in your neighborhood with door-to-door flyers and signs. If you have a car or truck, try a few ads in the newspaper to reach a wider audience.

Post a sign in the front yard while you are painting to advertise to people who drive by. Also, consider contacting a local sign company to purchase small aluminum signs with your name and telephone number that you can hang permanently on or near your completed houses for additional advertising.

Just as in fence painting, the only way to build a business is to have satisfied customers who will give you excellent recommendations. You have to bend over backwards, especially in the beginning, to do a thorough and neat job.

One great advantage of the house painting business is that you can turn this venture into a solid, lifetime career. Many large paint contractors started out as one-person, part-time operations. Then, they branched out by hiring employees and bidding on large commercial contract paint jobs for apartment or business buildings.

Idea

Pool Service

Job Description: Pool cleaning maintenance worker

Personal Traits Required: Cautious about safety around water and chemicals, and ability to do a thorough cleaning job

Experience Required: Previous pool cleaning experience required

Materials Required: Pool test kit

Supplemental Materials: Pool chemicals, pool toys and accessories

Marketing Method: Door-to-door flyer

Expected Wages: At least $5 per hour

Pool cleaning will be a viable business for you only if you live in the Sun Belt, but it can be quite lucrative. Pool cleaning is typically provided by professionals employed by large swimming pool companies. These professionals charge anywhere from $18 to $40 per visit. You should be able to clean a pool in two to three hours, so if you price your service at $10 to $15, you should be able to make money. Pool cleaning doesn't take much strength or experience to do a good job, so it's a good business for almost any teen.

Professional pool cleaners usually do the following on every visit:

1. Backwash the filter
2. Brush and vacuum the bottom and sides
3. Hand scrub the tile at the pool surface
4. Check the chemicals
5. Add the necessary chemicals, provided by the customer
6. Hose down the surrounding decking

Most professional services will clean pools only if the customer signs up for a long-term service contract. One-time-only cleaning is more trouble, and is therefore priced higher than regular service. You should do the same, offering weekly, twice monthly, and one-time-only prices. Ask to see the pool before you quote any prices. The sizes of backyard swimming pools don't vary that much—you should be able to do any of them in two to three hours. What will take you longer is the occasional backyard olympic-sized pool, or an unusually dirty pool.

Before you begin, get some experience operating pool filters and cleaning pools. You can acquire adequate experience in a very short time. If you don't have a pool, find a friend with one and practice a couple of times. Buy a pool care book at your local swimming pool store and study it thoroughly. You should be able to recognize problems with pool water, such as algae and unstable water, and be able to fix them. If one of your customers has a particularly unusual or stubborn water problem, take a sample of the pool water into any swimming pool supply store that sells chemicals; they usually provide a free service that analyzes water problems and recommends solutions. (They make their money on selling you the chemicals to fix the problem.) Know your own limitations. Some major water or equipment problems will be beyond your ability to fix; however, you should be able to spot problems and let your customers know about them immediately.

The only equipment you need is a full-service water test kit that checks for chlorine and pH balance (acidity vs. alkalinity). These kits are small and portable. Don't rely on the many different kinds you will find at your customers' homes. You want your OWN kit that you are familiar with and that will provide consistent results. Virtually all swimming pools are installed with their own cleaning hardware—skimmers, vacuum heads and brushes—so you won't have to lug any heavy equipment.

If you have a large enough business and a vehicle, you could also make money by selling swimming pool chemicals. Locate a wholesale supplier and buy in bulk. Many of the pool chemicals are dangerous and must be stored carefully. You *must* have a thorough understanding of how to use and store them properly.

You can also make money by offering a small line of fun pool accessories if you can find a wholesale or low-priced supplier. Sell these items while you are there cleaning; you have a captive audience. Pool stores make a very large profit on these items, and you can, too. Try selling fun accessories such as water basketball and volleyball sets, floating bars, floating lights and rafts. Check retail prices first before you set your own prices. You needn't drastically undercut local retail store prices in order to sell. Your customers will pay at least full retail price for the convenience of being able to buy them in their own home. *Plus,* these pool toys should be easy to sell. It's hard for customers to resist a fun new toy if you demonstrate it in their own pool. Don't go overboard buying a lot of inventory. Too much stock will be difficult to store and will cost you money up front. Just pick a few fun, distinctive items that are quick sellers.

Idea 9

Home Improvement— Safety and Energy Efficiency

Job Description: Home improvement technician

Personal Traits Required: Some mechanical aptitude

Experience Required: Depends upon service you provide. Some of the suggestions below are easy and can be performed by almost anyone. But the more complicated installations, such as attic insulation, take experience and knowledge.

Materials Required: Weather stripping, insulation batting, smoke detectors, etc.

Marketing Method: Door-to-door flyer or newspaper ads

Expected Wages: $5 to $8 per hour

Today's homeowner is much more safety and energy conscious than a few years ago. People are aware of what it takes to make their homes safe and energy efficient. Yet many of them don't take or have the time to perform simple safety and energy checks and improvements.

You can provide a comprehensive service that will improve your neighbors' homes and make your neighborhood a safer one. What you choose to include as part of your service is entirely up to you. This job is part SALES and part SERVICE. You can simply sell these items, such as weather stripping for doors and windows, or charge extra and perform a complete installation service. You may decide to include all the things on the list below as part of your business, or specialize in one or two products or services. The following list will give you some ideas:

Safety

▶ Fire extinguishers

▶ Smoke detectors

▶ Burglar alarms—There are many varieties of burglar alarms. You won't be able to install the more expensive, complicated variety that requires wiring throughout the customers' homes in the wall. But there are many simple alarms that can be easily installed. Check at a local hardware shop.

▶ Children's safety latches—These latches keep babies and toddlers out of drawers, cabinets and rooms—and also out of danger and mischief. Only older children and adults can operate the latches. Cabinet latches require a screwdriver or an electric drill to install.

▶ Fireproof safety deposit boxes for storing important family papers

▶ First aid kits

▶ Clearing downspouts of leaves and debris—service only

▶ Deadbolt locks—This takes some practice. You have to have some woodworking skills and experience installing locks before attempting this.

▶ Door chains

▶ Door peepholes—These are installed in wooden or metal doors, which takes some skill with a power drill. You'll need to practice before you attempt this for customers.

Energy Efficiency

▶ Weather stripping around doors and windows

▶ Putty around windows and doors

▶ Insulation blanket around hot water heater

▶ Attic insulation—Caution! Be sure to read up on proper attic insulation techniques. This is not a job for amateurs. You MUST know what you are doing. The wrong type or amount of insulation can do more harm than good. Also, many fiberglass insulation materials are difficult to handle—the glass splinters can harm your skin. The U.S. government has standards for proper attic insulation. Check with a local builder, hardware store or insulation materials supply company for information.

▶ Plastic insulating window covers

▶ Hoods for chimneys and/or roof turbine fans

▶ Automatic timers for the heating/cooling system— these devices turn the thermostat up or down at preset times and are quite simple to install.

▶ Watersaving shower heads

▶ Toilet adapters that cut down on water used for flushing

This is a partial list of what you might provide. Read everything you can about home safety and energy efficiency. For additional ideas, check around the community. Local utility companies usually have free brochures about energy-saving techniques. Check with the Red Cross or a local hospital to see if they have information about safety measures for the home. The fire department and police typically provide information or brochures. The library will also be a good source of information.

You can market your business by going around to your neighbors, but people can be suspicious of door-to-door home improvement and repair people. Try the door-to-door flyer. Remember, you will be providing a necessary and useful service, so emphasize that in your ad. One key selling point, if you decide to provide energy-saving products and installation, is that your customers will probably recoup the cost of your service by saving on their utility bills.

Idea

10

Shrub Maintenance

Job Description: Gardener/horticulturalist

Personal Traits Required: A green thumb

Experience Required: Knowledge of local plants

Materials Required: Fertilizer, gardening implements, pruning shears

Supplemental Materials Required: Insect and disease control devices

Marketing Method: Door-to-door flyer

Expected Wages: At least $5 per hour.

If you are in an area of the country where landscape shrubbery is a "big deal," such as the south central and south eastern states and California, *and* if you enjoy working outdoors with plants, then this would make a great job for you. Most larger towns and cities have regular maintenance services for lawns, such as Lawn Doctor or Chem Lawn. These companies provide a scheduled service for grass fertilization and weed and bug control. However, most of these companies don't provide a similar service for shrubbery and if they do, it is priced at least $40 per service call. Plus, these big companies don't supply what shrubbery REALLY needs on a regular basis—tender, loving care. If homeowners want the tough stuff done for them—weeding, soil cultivation, pruning or planting—they have to hire a gardener.

You could provide a regularly scheduled, complete service to take care of customers' landscape shrubbery at a price far less than the pros and still earn good money. The service could include some or all of the following:

1.   Fertilization at proper times of the year

2.   Weed control (this will probably involve getting down in the dirt and hand-pulling weeds)

3. Pruning and trimming shrubs and ground cover in shrub beds

4. Keeping grass out of shrub beds

5. Soil cultivation

6. Soil testing and balance–maintaining the proper pH and mineral levels for plants

IF you are an older teen, and IF you stay away from the more toxic chemicals, you also might consider including:

7. Insect control

8. Disease control

Caution: Chemicals used for control can be dangerous if handled improperly. Always check with an agriculture extension office or a local nursery to find the safest method of controlling insects and disease. If you are a younger teen, or if you aren't up to the safety measures required for handling chemicals, leave this part of the business to the pros.

You could also offer to plant and maintain annual flowers, bulbs and bushes. Charge at least $5 per hour for this. It's hard work, and you won't have much competition. The nurseries don't handle small plantings, and private gardeners are beyond the means of most homeowners.

To provide good service, you need to know everything you can about *local* plants, especially:

▶ What types of fertilizer are used for what types of plants, and when to apply them.

▶ What diseases are prevalent in the area, and how to diagnose and treat them.

▶ What insects come at what times of the year, types of plants they attack, and how to get rid of them.

You'll have to do plenty of reading or research to pick up this knowledge, but there's usually help available. Local nurseries provide free diagnosis for plant problems. Most states have agricultural extension offices in every county to give advice, not just for farmers but also for homeowners with horticultural questions and problems. This service is free, and offices are usually glad to help. Many community colleges offer short courses on landscape maintenance and problems.

Many fertilizers, bug and disease sprays are suitable for a wide variety of plants and conditions. If you spray BEFORE you see problems, you can avoid most bug and disease infestations. Select the best quality chemicals available; ask your local nursery for their recommendations. Buy in bulk whenever possible. Many chemicals and fertilizers can be purchased in large quantities at a discount at large farm stores in rural areas. Or, check with a friendly local nursery to see if you qualify for a discount for quantity purchases.

Once you have a good working knowledge of how to care for plants in your area, then develop an all-purpose maintenance schedule for a typical home. Practice on your own or a friend's shrubbery to see how much time and material you need. Base your price estimates upon material expenses, plus your labor. You can handle most landscape problems with regular and prompt application of fertilizers and pest controls; however, some problems will crop up that will need treatment between regularly scheduled visits. When preparing your price estimate, you'll need to budget a certain percentage of your time to cover problem calls, plus a percentage to handle "overhead" time, the time you spend on bookkeeping, answering the phone, calling on prospective customers, advertising, and travel between customers.

For example, after you thoroughly understand the products you need to maintain healthy shrubbery plus how long it takes to apply those products, prepare a price estimate like this:

Fertilizer	$ 4
Bug spray	3
Disease control spray	3
Two hours labor @ $5 per hr.	10
Overhead time* (1 hr. @ $5)	5
TOTAL COST PER VISIT	$25

*This is your estimate of how much "overhead" time you need to organize your business, handle telephone calls, advertise and keep records per customer.

Depending upon conditions in your area of the country, regular maintenance might be needed monthly, every six weeks, or four times per year. You could price your service on an annual basis, or per application. You'll need to develop a pricing plan. Here's a sample advertising message:

For as low as just $25 per month during the growing season, The Shrub Doc will keep your landscape looking its best. We provide a complete maintenance service to keep your shrubbery healthy and bug and disease free. Free estimates upon request.

Thus, you could establish $25 as your minimum for an average yard, but reserve the right to charge more for larger or weed-infested yards. In addition to a pricing plan, you need to establish a payment policy, such as six equal monthly installment payments during the growing season, or payment immediately after a service call.

Measure all fertilizers and chemicals properly. Don't overdo it! Applying too much can sometimes do more damage than not applying any at all. Plus, you need to keep a very close eye on costs. Careful measurement will ensure you don't spend more than you budget for gardening products.

If you plan to include bug and disease control as part of your business, you'll need to buy proper applicators. If you use chemical sprays, it's a good idea to use a different applicator for each type of spray. Even a speck of residue left from another product in the bottom of the applicator could become deadly when mixed with another. You will also save time by not having to do the exremely thorough cleaning required with changing chemicals in an applicator.

If you plan on using chemicals, you need to know safe and proper handling and storage techniques. Certain sprays can be extremely toxic and potentially harmful to your health if used over a period of time. Get proper advice from local nurseries or a local agricultural extension office on product safety. For safety's sake:

▶ Use a mask while spraying.

▶ Substitute less toxic chemicals whenever possible.

▶ Wear a long-sleeved shirt, long pants, socks and heavy-duty shoes to reduce your exposure to chemicals.

▶ Always wear eye protectors and gloves when handling the chemicals.

Idea

Garage Cleaning

Job Description: Custodial worker

Personal Traits Required: A penchant for neatness and organization

Experience Required: None

Materials Required: Large broom, hose (these are usually provided by the homeowner), rags, glass cleaner, all-purpose cleaner, short-handled broom or portable vacuum, bucket, garbage bags, oil and grease cleaner for cement floors

Supplemental Materials: Shelving, paint & brushes, pegboard, pegboard hooks

Marketing Method: Door-to-door flyer

Expected Wages: $5 per hour

One of the most hated, feared and postponed jobs in any home is cleaning the garage. While many homeowners keep the inside of their house immaculate, the majority of garages have months or years of dust and debris accumulated in corners. You could cure many a homeowner's blues by offering a very special garage cleaning service.

One advantage to this service is that you won't have much competition. Most maids and cleaning services won't set foot inside a garage. The key to building a good business is to make your service very special—you can't just offer a quick dust and sweep. You must be very particular about the cleaning you provide, and go that extra mile, to make sure everything sparkles when you are through. The homeowner should be able to inspect and say *"wow!"* when you're finished.

A thorough cleaning should include at least the following:

▶ Remove all objects from shelves and wash the shelves.

▶ Dust or wash the tops of containers.

▶ Pick up everything that looks like trash—old greasy rags, newspapers, loose screws on the floor. Put all the trash in a trash bag, but give it to the homeowner before you leave. Don't *ever* throw anything away until he or she first has a chance to inspect the "garbage."

▶ Organize the shelves in a meaningful way, if at all possible. For example, put all the automotive items together, and put paint and repair equipment, sporting goods, etc., on separate shelves so the garage is not one big jumble. You might want to ask the homeowner for guidance.

▶ Remove cobwebs and dust fuzzies from corners and the ceiling.

70

▶ Remove oil and grease stains from the garage floor, using a special solvent made for cement.

▶ Clean glass windows.

▶ Sweep and hose down the garage floor. If the homeowner's hose won't reach the garage from an outdoor spigot, then bring your own hose or use a bucket and broom.

Ask the homeowner to be there while you are cleaning. Prepare a short list of questions to ask before you begin, so you don't bother customers as you work. Experience will tell you what you need to know during the cleaning process, but before you begin, at least:

1. Ask homeowners to remove all vehicles from the garage.

2. Briefly describe the service you provide.

3. Inform customers that you won't be throwing anything away, but will put all items that appear to be trash in bags for their inspection later.

4. Ask if they have any preferences as to how the shelves should be organized.

5. Ask if they have any items they don't want you to touch or move.

6. If you find any odds and ends that don't appear to belong anywhere, tell customers you will lay these aside, and ask for a place to put them so they won't get lost. (Don't end up with a huge pile of "odds and ends." Do your best to find a place for everything.)

A good, thorough garage cleaning should take you two to three hours. As you gain experience, your time will speed up. Every time you clean a garage, follow the same steps in the same order. Take a checklist with you to make sure you don't forget anything. If you have standard garages in your neighborhood, you could offer a fixed price of, say, $15 to $20 for a two-car garage. If garages vary, ask homeowners if you can see the garage first before you give them an estimate.

The best way to reach homeowners is with a door-to-door flyer. Make sure you describe all the special touches you provide, so customers don't think you will simply come in and sweep the floor. Garage cleaning is something that should be done at least once every three months. One way to keep your business growing is to make sure you get repeat customers. Keep your clients satisfied, and keep track of when you cleaned for each customer. When two months have passed, call clients for a repeat cleaning.

You can boost your revenue by selling garage organization paraphernalia. If you are at all handy with carpentry, and if a garage needs it, offer to build shelving or install pegboard. One pesky item that's always taking up too much space is a bicycle. Bicycle hooks are inexpensive and can be quickly mounted on the ceiling. It should be easy to sell these things right after you clean, particularly if you do an outstanding job of cleaning. Price the installation service so that it covers the cost of materials plus earns you at least $5 per hour.

Idea
12

Lawn Service

Job Description: Lawn care technician

Personal Traits Required: Safety conscious and fussy about your finished work

Experience Required: Mowing and trimming lawns

Materials Required: Lawn mower, grass trimmer, lawn edger (for certain parts of the country with creeping grass such as bermuda), extension cord if you have any electric equipment, blower or long-handled broom, lawn and leaf trash bags.

Marketing Method: Door-to-door flyer

Expected Wages: $5 per hour

Do you ever wonder why some people are willing to pay a professional gardener $50 and more to cut grass, but teenagers usually get paid less than minimum wage? The secret is professionalism. Most kids don't take the time or have the patience to do an outstanding job cutting grass and cleaning up afterward. Many adults complain that teens leave too many "mohawks," rows of grass missed by the mower or unevenly scalped, and that teens don't clean up well when they're done. Professionals guarantee their service and always do a great job. They take pride in their work; it's not just a way to earn pocket change.

You can achieve that same professionalism and get decent pay for lawn care work, too. It's all in your approach, your attention to detail, your willingness to satisfy customers, and some professional marketing tactics. Here are some tips:

1. **Practice, practice, practice** on your own lawn and those of friends. Have adults inspect your work carefully before you attempt to sell your service.

2. **Keep your equipment in good repair.** Pay special attention to keeping the blades on your mower sharp. Dull blades cut grass unevenly and slow down your work.

3. **Take time to become a lawn care "expert."** Get recommendations from a local nursery or horticulturalist on the length to trim grass for different times of the year. Learn to spot turf problems, such as fungus, disease or insects that destroy lawns, and make recommendations about curing these problems.

4. **Be *sure* to clean up after yourself.** This is one of the biggest complaints about teen grass clippers. You can blow most of the grass off sidewalks as you mow by running the mower lightly over the sidewalk. Finish the job neatly by sweeping or using an electric blower. Bag all the grass clippings, unless specifically asked not to by the homeowner.

If you are planning on using your parents' lawn equipment, take responsibility for supplying your own fuel. Pay for repairs and maintenance out of your earnings. Your parents' equipment should be available for them to use when they need it. Better yet, do all your family yardwork in partial payment for the loan of the family lawn equipment.

If you can provide a premium service, you can charge a premium price. Check the going rates in your neighborhood for teenage mowers, then check what professionals charge for the same job. You should be able to price your service somewhere in between *provided* you do a fantastic job. You will have to be the *best* at lawn care in your neighborhood, and guarantee complete customer satisfaction. Boost your professionalism by:

1. **Using snazzy advertising**—a well-drawn, well-thought-out advertising flyer dropped off at every door.

2. **Setting appointments for lawn care in advance,** and always showing up on time, barring rain.

3. **Dressing well.** Wear neat and clean pants or shorts and a shirt. Keep your shirt on, even in hot weather. Better yet, wear a T-shirt printed with your name or company name and phone number. This will impress your clients and perhaps get you some extra business from people driving by.

4. **Talking with your clients.** Ask them what they are particularly fussy about. Before you leave, make sure they are satisfied with your work.

5. **Using a professional business card.** Leave this with your customers for passing on to a friend or neighbor.

6. **Being confident when talking to your clients.** Look them straight in the eye. If you have any lawn care recommenda-

tions or have spotted some disease or insect problems, don't be afraid to discuss them. Your customers will appreciate your professionalism.

7. Checking on sprinkler systems. If you live in a part of the country where automatic sprinkler systems are used, check with the homeowner for location of the spray heads. You can do hundreds of dollars' worth of damage by mowing over expensive sprinkler heads.

8. Advertising. While you are mowing, stick up a sign in the yard with your name and phone number, so people passing by have a chance to contact you later for service.

Many teens overlook one way to boost business: bidding on larger lawn jobs. If you have small business, church, apartment or community buildings close by, consider stopping by and making a sales pitch. Have a price ready to quote for them and provide references. If you have a pickup truck, you can bid on jobs all over the city.

Neighborhood Ventures— Inside Work

13. Latchkey Service
14. Laundry/Ironing Service
15. Super Baby-Sitter—Parents' Night Out
16. Super Baby-Sitter—Parents' Weekend Out
17. Super Baby-Sitter—Special Afternoons
18. House Sitting
19. Party Helpers
20. Window Washing
21. House Cleaning
22. Birthday Party Service
23. Home Bakery

This section has ideas for indoor work around the neighborhood. While some of the outside jobs in the previous section can be performed only during the summer in many parts of the country, the ideas in this section are suitable for steady work year-round. Most of them don't require any special equipment or transportation, as long as you have an adult to round up a few basic supplies. Also, this group of ideas seems to have the greatest market potential. The need for these services is growing at a tremendous pace along with three general trends in our society: 1) more women and mothers are entering the work force, 2) more people are healthy and working past the age of sixty, and 3) people desire more leisure time. These three trends won't be peaking anytime soon. So, scout around, find your market niche, and go after it!

Idea
13

Latchkey Service

Job Description: Child care/housekeeping

Personal Traits Required: You must love children and be able to establish a warmth and rapport with them. Also, you need to have a great sense of responsibility for the children in your care.

Experience Required: Previous baby-sitting experience

Materials Required: None

Marketing Method: Door-to-door flyer

Expected Wages: $4 to $6 per hour

Society as a whole and working parents are becoming quite concerned about their "latchkey children," children who return home from school to an empty house, wearing their housekeys around their necks. ABC Television News, in a fairly recent report, estimated that there were between seven to ten million latchkey children in the United States. Many times, these children are too old to be enrolled in commercial day care centers. But either the parents or the children themselves don't want kids to be left alone in the house until the parents return from work. A few day care centers do offer after-school care, but many of these services have serious limitations. The most serious for working parents is day care center closing hours. The majority offer care only until 6:00 p.m., and some parents cannot get there by closing time. Also, space is limited and most take children only through the lower primary grades. Many communities don't offer any type of after-school day care at all, leaving the "latchkey children" to fend for themselves at a very young age.

The ideal service would put you in the children's house when they return home from school. Or you could meet them at their school and walk home with them. However, as an older student, your school hours are probably later than theirs. Some high schools have flexible scheduling that allows you to attend earlier in the morning for an earlier dismissal time. Even if your schedule won't permit you to greet the kids as they get home from school, you can still provide a valuable service if you reach a home by a designated hour every day and stay with the children until the parents return home from work, from 4:30 to 6:30 daily, for example.

Pricing your service can be complicated. Your fees will ultimately depend on the hours, the number of children, and the service you provide. Aim at undercutting the prices of your competition, the professional day care centers. The going rate for after-school care is anywhere from $25 to $50 per week per child. If you locate parents with two or more children, and price your service in the $20 range per week per child, both of you would be getting a good deal. You could charge less per child if you offered the service in your home and had more children. Up to five children shouldn't be too difficult to handle for short stretches in the afternoon, provided your family doesn't mind. Or, suggest to prospective clients that they double up with another family and share the baby-sitting fee, perhaps alternating houses weekly. Then you could really lower the rates per child and still earn $4 to $6 per hour. See the example below:

Example
Jan's Baby-Sitting Service

Two Fletcher children: Martin & Amanda	**$24**	per week
Three Smith children: Joby, Andrea and Kevin	**$36**	per week
Total weekly pay	**$60**	per week

Five children total, $12 per child

Schedule: From 4 to 6:30 Monday through Friday, 12.5 total hours

Hourly Wage: $60 divided by 12.5 hours = $4.80 per hour

Schedule: Alternate homes, first week at Fletchers', second week at Smiths'.

If you are going to work for an individual family and you want to earn a premium price, offer special services as part of your "package." School-age children do not require constant supervision, so you will have some time to do light tasks around the house while you are there. Some suggestions:

▶ Preparing the dinner meal

▶ Light laundry

▶ Kitchen cleanup

▶ Vacuuming/dusting

▶ Bedmaking

You can't be too ambitious with extra services and still provide quality care, so don't go overboard. Don't sign up to keep the entire house clean *and* watch the children. This would be a superhuman assignment that no one could do well. But providing just one special service regularly, such as starting supper every evening, could be a godsend for a parent and make your fee well worth it.

Spend some time interviewing parents before you begin work. Check out the ground rules of the household, what the parents do and do not allow. Get their attitudes on snacks, and when they can be offered. Ask the parents what they want their kids to be doing. After-school afternoons might be strictly for homework, or the parents may allow television. If TV is OK, check with the parents if anything is off limits. Ask what chores, if any, the children are responsible for before their parents arrive home, such as taking out garbage, making beds, cleaning their rooms, etc. Find out the parents' policy on visiting friends, how far the children may go from the house after school and for how long. Take good notes and keep them handy; or, better yet, post the rules in a convenient spot to avoid arguments with the children.

You are providing a service to relieve parents' anxieties and help them while they are out earning money. Most working parents with kids face constant telephone interruptions from their kids after school. So interrupt the parents at work ONLY in case of a true emergency, and don't allow the children to place calls, either. You should be able to handle most situations without bothering parents at work.

Remember, in all your work, be a professional! Your key to success will be reliability. If you can't be there on a given day, locate a suitable substitute. Make sure your clients know your "sub." But don't make a habit of using substitutes.

One of the greatest advantages of this business idea is that you will have virtually *no* competition. Most parents vastly prefer having their children safe in their own home rather than at a day care center. Another great advantage is that you won't have to spend much time advertising or keeping records. All you need is one regular customer to earn a good wage; that customer will probably be a long-term client.

The most effective form of advertising will be door-to-door flyers in your neighborhood. State any special skills, services or activities you provide along with your basic child care service. Have your list of good baby-sitting references handy when the parents call to inquire. You should provide references, even if the parents don't think to ask.

Once you begin your work, make sure you have certain basic information at your fingertips at all times:

▶ Parents' work locations, telephone numbers and addresses

▶ Name of each parent's boss or supervisor in case of emergency

▶ Name, address and phone number of children's doctor

▶ Phone number of close friend or relative who might be available to come over to assist in case of emergency

▶ Phone number of poison control center

▶ Information on special diets or medications

A sample baby-sitter's checklist is included on the next page. You should use this form, or make up one of your own, for all the baby-sitting job ideas in this section.

One word of caution: if you watch children in your home on a regular basis, you may fall under state child welfare regulations for day care centers. For example, in Texas, if you take *any* amount of children into your home (even one!), you must register with the state as a "registered family home." The fee is $35, and you must follow state guidelines on fire safety, nutrition and health for the children in your care. You are also subject to inspection by state welfare officials to ensure you follow the guidelines. This is not all bad, of course. It will give you added credibility if you advertise as a state-licensed operation. Many home day care operators don't bother to register, and are subject to fines and prosecution. Check with local child welfare officials to find out your obligations.

Baby-Sitter's Checklist

Father's name: _____

Work address: _____

_____
(Company name)

Work phone: _____

Supervisor's
name/phone: _____
(For emergency use only)

Mother's name: _____

Work address: _____

_____
(Company name)

Work phone: _____

Supervisor's
name/phone: _____
(For emergency use only)

Names and ages of children: _____

_____

Children's doctor:

Name: _____

Address: _____

Phone: _____

Emergency numbers

Neighbor or close relative— Name: _____

Phone: _____

Alternate neighbor/relative—Name: _____

Phone: _____

Poison control center: _____

Fire: _____ Police: _____

Special diet information: _____

Medications: _____

Snacks (Time/type): _____

Other instructions: _____

_____

_____

Idea
14

Laundry/Ironing Service

Job Description: Clothing care technician

Personal Traits Required: You must enjoy working alone, and keep motivated to finish your work without supervision.

Experience Required: Operating laundry equipment

Materials Required: None if performed in your clients' homes. If done at your house: a washer & dryer, laundry soap, laundry baskets, bleach, and softener.

Supplemental Materials: Iron, starch, ironing board, spray bottle

Marketing Method: Door-to-door flyer

Expected Wages: $4 to $6 per hour

This service can be a golden opportunity for you, as there is virtually no competition. If you are looking for a job that no one else is doing, or doing well, pick this one. For the busy working person or couple, laundry is the last thing they want to do in their limited spare time. There are very few alternatives available for people who want laundry done for them. Dry cleaners don't usually do general laundry such as socks, towels, and underwear. They will launder dress shirts and blouses, and the going rate these days is around $1.25 per shirt. If you can find a cleaning company to do laundry, they charge approximately $1.25 per pound. At this rate, the average family wash could cost well over $30. Many people who have tried laundry services have had fair to poor luck with them. Laundry services won't accept individualized instructions for special garments; many items come back with holes, buttons missing, or lingerie melted from the high-heat dryers found in commercial establishments. Lately, maid services have become quite popular, but the vast majority refuse to do any kind of laundry other than sheets and towels.

There are two basic methods you can use to run a laundry and/or ironing service:

Method 1: Out of your home You can arrange to have your customers drop off laundry in laundry bags or baskets at your house and pick up the clean, folded laundry the next day. This method will give you more flexibility with your schedule than if you did the laundry at your customer's house, and you probably would be able to handle more customers. However, doing other people's laundry at your house might interfere with your family's activities and subject your washer and dryer to unacceptable wear and tear. You would then be responsible for machine repairs and washing supplies, which could get expensive. The utility bills for extra gas, electricity and water could easily run $10 per month per customer.

Method 2: Out of your customer's home The other method would be to do laundry at your customer's house after school, preferably while the family is away. (It could take you considerably longer if there are small children present.) By doing laundry at their house, you can provide more individualized service. You have the advantage of being able to use their equipment and supplies, which also cuts your costs.

It takes approximately ten to twenty minutes to sort laundry and thirty to forty minutes for each cycle of the washer and dryer. Therefore, to do a typical family's wash, consisting of four to five washloads, should take you three to four hours. You could easily arrange to do this in one or two afternoons after school. To avoid the wage and hour issue, price this as a package service. It is extremely difficult to estimate beforehand just how long laundry will take. Some older equipment takes much longer to run a cycle. You could start by charging a fixed rate of $15 to $20 per week. Or, you could charge a flat fee of $5 per load of clothes. This should put you well under your competition and earn you around $5 per hour. You will have to charge more if your customer has older laundry machines, lots of kids, or special needs such as washing diapers. Practice timing a complete family wash at your house a few times to get an accurate time estimate before you price your service.

In order to offer a professional service, here are some special features you might include:

▶ Strip bed linens, wash and put back on beds. This won't take you any extra time because you can do this while the laundry machines are running.

▶ Fold all clothes neatly (including matching the socks) and put them in a central spot, such as the bed in the master bedroom, when finished. Don't offer to put them all away, as this will take a great deal of extra time, and you might misplace important items for your customers.

▶ Remove all towels from their racks, wash and put back.

▶ Provide special care for laundry that dry cleaners won't handle, such as hand washing of nylons or use of special products such as bleach, sanitizer and/or softeners.

Here are some tips that will make your job easier and save you time and trouble.

▶ First, separate laundry into piles according to the type of care the clothes need. You should do a separate load for whites, colors, darks, permanent press, and if your customer asks you to, for women's lingerie. Instructions for washing each type of clothing should be on the clothing labels, washing machine or on the detergent.

▶ Be sure to ask customers to demonstrate their equipment before you start, as well as any special products they want used.

▶ The first load(s) should be the one with the most folding work, such as dark socks. Your last load should be the easiest to fold and/or put away, so you don't have to spend any more time at the customer's house than you have to.

▶ If you aren't sure about the proper washing temperature or method for a garment, put it aside and ask the customer later. The washing/drying method should be printed on a label inside the garment, but labels are often missing. The last thing you want to do is ruin your customer's clothes by shrinking them or having non-colorfast clothing stain an entire washload.

▶ To save time, be sure to start a new load the minute the washing machine stops. It's very easy to forget. Dryers have buzzers to signal you, but not washers. Carry a small pocket timer to remind you.

▶ Be sure to take out permanent press items the instant they finish washing and again when they finish tumbling in the dryer. If they sit even for a few minutes, the clothes will look as if a truck ran over them! Make sure you use the permanent press cycle on the washer and the wrinkle guard feature on the dryer if these are available.

▶ Measure all laundry powders and liquids carefully, following the instructions on the package. Some are highly concentrated! You could ruin a machine by an overdose of soap.

You could also offer an ironing service in conjunction with your laundry service. It is extremely difficult to find someone to come into a home just to do ironing. The demand is greatest for men's dress shirts. Dry cleaners charge about $1.25 for cleaning and pressing shirts. It is rare to find one that will *just* do pressing. Pressing charges run about half the price of cleaning and pressing; a men's dress shirt is typically around seventy-five cents. It takes five to ten minutes per shirt to do a really good job. Charge at least forty cents per dress shirt, and twenty-five cents for smaller items such as shorts, napkins, and handkerchiefs. These rates would not earn you minimum wage if done by themselves, but you will have some time between loads to iron. You could charge by the piece, or a flat fee, such as an extra $10 per week for ironing. This will depend upon your customer's needs. Stay away from pressing expensive fabrics such as silk, suede or linen; it's very easy to ruin them. Even the pros make mistakes on these. Also, avoid pressing garments with complicated construction, such as suits. You might want to restrict your ironing to cotton or cotton blend fabrics to avoid problems. If you are going to set rules on what you will and will not iron, explain them to your client before you begin the service, to avoid misunderstanding.

Make sure you use a clean iron. Buildup on the bottom can stain clothing. Check the temperature setting, and iron each fabric type separately using the appropriate heat setting. Using a spray bottle of water is the fastest way to smooth out wrinkles, much quicker than the mist on a spray/steam iron. Be sure to ask customers if they want any garments starched. If so, go easy at first. Remember, ironing is much more difficult to do properly than simply washing and folding. Practice at home before you charge money for this service.

If you offer ironing as a separate service, you'll have to charge enough to earn at least $5 per hour. That means your prices for ironing alone will be higher than if you were also doing a customer's laundry. If it takes you ten minutes to do a good job on a dress shirt, you will need to charge 85 cents to iron it. Ask around your neighborhood to see what people are willing to pay for a good ironing service, and check to see if your price is lower than the professional dry cleaners.

You won't need a lot of fancy advertising to earn good part-time wages in this business. All you'll be able to handle is one to four regular customers per week, which could net you $20 to $80 per week. The most effective form of advertising is flyers circulated door to door.

Before you begin service with a new client, ask about special instructions, care or products the client wants you to use. You can use the sample form on the next page, or invent your own. Ask your client to fill out such a form every laundry day, to avoid problems and miscommunication:

Laundry Service Instructions

Check below the separate loads you need washed:

_____ Whites   Bleach? Circle Yes No

_____ Color

_____ Permanent press

_____ Dark

_____ Lingerie/gentle

_____ Handwash Specify handwash items: _____
_____

_____ Other Specify type: _____

State laundry products you prefer:

_____

Special instructions on laundry: (*Note:* Garments requiring special care should be clearly marked)

_____

_____

_____

_____

IRONING

Check below items you want ironed. If you want starch, circle Y.

___ Men's dress shirts Y   ___ Ladies' blouses Y

___ Men's casual shirts Y   ___ Ladies' casual shirts Y

___ Men's pants Y   ___ Ladies' pants Y

___ Men's shorts Y   ___ Ladies' shorts Y

___ Children's pants Y   ___ Children's shirts Y

___ Children's dresses Y   ___ Children's shorts Y

Other: _____

_____

_____

Idea

15

Super Baby-Sitter— Parents' Night Out

Job Description: Baby-sitter

Personal Traits Required: Outgoing personality and good rapport with children

Experience Required: Previous baby-sitting

Materials Required: This depends on how you plan to entertain your youngsters

Marketing Method: Door-to-door flyer

Expected Wages: $5 to $10 per hour

Traditional baby-sitting certainly wouldn't make it on a list of high profit entrepreneurial ideas. The wages and hours are lousy. Baby-sitting rarely, if ever, pays minimum wage. The going rates range from $1 to $3.50 per hour for teenagers. The only way to make good money at it is to offer a professional, specialized service.

Parents' Night Out is a regularly scheduled baby-sitting service given at your home on a specific night for a specific set of hours. For example, you could offer this every Friday night from 5:30 to 10:00. This would not meet everyone's needs, but many couples would love to have a night out they could count on. One person alone could handle up to five children for that period. Over that number, you might need to bring in a friend for help. (It might be a good idea for you to have a pool of friends available to help out with crowds.) The important ingredient for a high-quality service is reliability. If you set it up for Friday night, you must offer it *every* Friday night. If an emergency comes up and you can't work on one of your scheduled evenings, as a professional, you should arrange a competent substitute. If you start cancelling out on regular customers, they'll quickly find another sitter to take your place.

Charge a flat fee for the service, rather than quoting an hourly wage. If you charge $7 per child for a five hour evening, and have five children, you would earn $7 per hour. This would still be less for a parent than hiring a regular baby-sitter. You could offer a discount on two or more children from the same family.

If you want to sell a high-quality, professional service, and charge a premium price, you need to offer something special for your customers. Here are some ideas:

▶ If you have a VCR, rent children's movies.

▶ Offer nutritious snacks, such as popcorn.

▶ Have preplanned activities such as games, singing or crafts. Parents particularly enjoy having their children come home with artwork or handicrafts.

▶ Dress up in whimsical clothing to entertain the children, such as a clown suit.

▶ Offer party favors or small, personalized gifts to take home.

Besides the special services or activities you provide, try to acquire some extra skills that will help you be a better baby-sitter. Most communities offer courses such as CPR training, first aid, and baby-sitting skills for little or no cost. If you do have some special training, be sure to announce it in your advertising.

It's important to know what the parents expect while you are watching their children. Develop a standard questionnaire, and make copies for all of your parents. You can modify the form printed at the end of Idea #13, substituting parents' whereabouts during the evening for their work information. Make sure all parents fill out the form for every session, before they leave for the evening.

The best form of advertising is probably the door-to-door flyer. Many parents complain that their baby-sitters are never available, and cancel at the last minute. So, if you can provide a service on a regularly scheduled night, you will probably find more customers than you can handle. If you do a good job, word-of-mouth advertising by satisfied customers will build up your business. Try to sign your customers up for a long-term contract, on a monthly basis. This should make your planning easier and save on advertising expenses.

Another idea along the same vein would be to offer parents a "Saturday Shopping Special." You could provide the same type of program as described above for a fixed set of hours during the daytime on Saturday, so parents can get away for shopping or errands. There are definite advantages for you, in that the hours might be more suitable for both you and your family. Going shopping with small children is next to impossible; neither the adults nor the children enjoy it. This would be a very valuable service on a day when it is difficult or impossible to find suitable day care.

Idea
16

Super Baby–Sitter— Parents' Weekend Out

Job Description: Overnight baby-sitting and light housekeeping

Personal Traits Required: Mature sense of responsibility and good rapport with children

Experience Required: Previous baby-sitting experience *required*

Materials Required: These will vary according to the services you provide and ages of the children.

Marketing Method: Door-to-door flyer

Expected Wages: Less than minimum wage per hour, which includes sleeping hours, but more than most part-time jobs. See below.

Here is a service that everyone with children seems to want but nobody can find—someone to watch their children while they get away for a special weekend. This business isn't recommended for the younger teenager because the responsibilities are too great, but it could be the perfect opportunity for the older teenager to make money.

It's difficult to set a price for this service; there isn't an "industry standard," and very few people do this on a regular basis. You can't really charge per hour, because you will be sleeping for several hours during that time. To charge from $75 to $125 for a weekend (from Friday night to Sunday evening) seems reasonable, but in reality your fee will depend upon the number of children, the demand, and your customers' ability to pay. If you charged minimum wage, which is currently $3.35, for a 48-hour weekend, your price would zoom up to $161. This would be beyond most families' means. Keep in mind that you will be working only twenty to thirty hours per weekend, the work can be easy and fun, and you will be providing a very necessary service.

Interview the parents well in advance of the weekend, so you have a clear idea what they expect in the way of activities and meals. They should provide you with a menu for the weekend and point out the location of the ingredients. Or, it might be easier for you to provide your own groceries and cook recipes you are familiar with. In that case, charge extra for the food. You also need to know who the children are allowed to play with, and where they are allowed to go. Check with the parents about any limits they have set for their children's behavior. Children sometimes try to take advantage of a sitter. "My mommy always lets me stay up until 11:30," or "Dad always feeds me chocolate bars for breakfast on Saturdays," for example. Try to get an idea of the bedtime and breakfast routine, and any scheduled activities the children have. If the children have appointments across town and you don't drive, make sure the parent has arranged transportation and you know exactly who will be providing it and when the children will return. Ask parents to fill out a form like the one in Idea #13, modifying it to delete work information and substituting parents' location for the weekend.

Find new customers by posting ads or business cards at the library, local day care centers and pediatricians' offices.

The key to a successful service business is word-of-mouth advertising and repeat customers. You want to do everything you can to demonstrate that your service is superior. The best testimonial to that is happy children and a clean and tidy house when the parents return. That will take work and planning before you ever set foot in the house. Before you begin your weekend, prepare a list of fun activities appropriate to the ages of the children. Check with your public library; they have lots of activity books for kids. Two hours before the parents are scheduled to return, round up all the kids and get them to pitch in to "super clean" the house.

Idea

17

Super Baby-Sitter— Special Afternoons

Job Description: Child development/education

Personal Traits Required: Outgoing personality and ability to communicate well with children

Experience Required: Previous baby-sitting

Materials Required: Depends upon type of afternoon you offer; for example, simple workbooks, songbooks, handicraft items

Marketing Technique: Door-to-door flyer

Expected Wages: $5 to $20 per hour

Parents, whether they are working or not, like to have their children participate in a regular program of fun, imaginative activities. You can organize one or more "special afternoons" for the neighborhood children in your home after you finish school. The type of service you provide will depend totally upon your skills, interests, and the ages of the children.

The idea here is to charge a reasonable fee for a number of children. How many you can handle will depend on your abilities and the ages of the children, but for short stretches in the afternoon, you might be able to handle up to ten kids. Some ideas of special afternoons might include:

- afternoons in the park
- handicrafts
- games
- story time
- puppetry
- dramatics, plays
- singing, dancing, rhythm
- education, such as reading readiness, phonics, math
- *light* exercise classes
- kiddie cooking classes
- etiquette and manners
- diet, food and nutrition

Instead of offering the same type of activity each week, you could provide a varied program including some or all of the above, but your service might be easier to sell if you specialize in one of these areas. *Don't* offer any type of strenuous physical education or gymnastics because of the liability involved should one of the children get hurt. You are responsible for the safety and well-being of the children under your care. Any activity like aerobics or gymnastics or athletic dancing is prone to accidents. Even cooking can be dangerous—keep small children away from knives, blenders, mixers, hot stove tops and ovens. A lawsuit from an angry parent over an injury could wipe out your and your family's savings. Insurance to protect you from liability would cost more than you could afford, and you probably couldn't qualify for a policy, anyway. The best bet is to *stay away* from any activities that could be dangerous *in any way* for the children.

You could set up a regular program one afternoon a week, say from 4:00 to 5:30. For example, if you charged $1.50 per child and had ten children, you would earn $10 per hour, less any material expenses. If you have a lot of expenses for materials, you might want to charge an additional registration and/or supplies fee. In that case, you could give the children a workbook or other materials they can take home and share with their parents. Any fee up to $5 per week per child would be reasonable for the combination of child care and education. Parents will feel more comfortable that they are getting something for their money if their children bring home something. If you teach a singing and rhythm class, buy songbooks or photocopy the list of songs you are teaching the children. Avoid giving parents the idea that this is just routine baby-sitting. It should be fun, it should be entertaining, but it should be educational as well. The children should be able to show something for the time they spend with you.

An example of a simple business plan for a children's cooking class is shown below.

Example
Pat's Cooking for Fun Class

Six one-hour cooking lessons on
preparing nutritious snacks
six Wednesday afternoons from 4:00 to 5:00
for children ages 5 to 7

Estimated enrollment: 8 children

Estimated material expenses: $5 per child

Fee: $18 + $5 material expenses = $23 per child

Estimate of profit:	8 children times $23	$184
	Less advertising costs	10
	Less material expense	40

Total profit $134

Estimate of work hours:	6	classroom hours
	8	hour organizing, preparing, advertising

Total work hours 14

Estimate of hourly wage:
  $134 divided by 14 hours = $9.57 per hr.

In this example, Pat plans to advertise using door-to-door flyers. $10 is the quote from the local printer to photocopy 200 hand-drawn flyers for distribution in her neighborhood. She plans on demonstrating the preparation of simple, nutritious snacks children can make without using sharp knives or utensils, and without using the stove or oven. Based on the recipes she has selected in advance, $40 is her estimate of grocery expenses for the class. She will cut down on costs by borrowing her family's kitchen utensils.

A recommended form of advertising is door-to-door flyers in your neighborhood. Check with local schools to see if you could put up posters, and speak with school teachers for the age group you want to teach, promoting your class. Be very specific about what you will be offering, the age group, time, and fees. If you have any special qualifications, list those in the ad. It would help for this type of ad to be colorful, with artwork and decorations that will appeal to children.

Because you will be imparting special skills to children, and because you aren't with them for extended periods, this type of service usually does not fall under state regulations for home day care. Normally, there's no need to register with the state or pay any fees. Check with local child welfare officials for the regulations in your area.

Idea
18

House Sitting

Job Description: Home security service
Personal Traits Required: You must have a high level of safety awareness. Because you are caring for someone else's home, you must be extra careful when checking the house and keeping doors and windows locked.

Experience Required: None

Materials Required: None

Marketing Method: Door-to-door flyer

Expected Wages: $5 and up per hour

House sitting is not a new concept. This is a service that watches over a house while the occupants are away on vacation or business. Many people offer house sitting services, which usually include some or all of the following activities:

▶ Watering plants
▶ Pet care
▶ Routine checking of the exterior and/or interior of the house
▶ Picking up mail and newspapers
▶ Lawn maintenance

▶ Watering lawns and shrubs

▶ Letting in repair or cleaning people on a pre-arranged schedule

The price for this service ranges anywhere from $30 to $100 per week and up, depending upon the community and the services included. One of the reasons it can be expensive is that house sitters often have expensive advertising costs for the yellow pages or newspapers. Also, house sitters usually drive in from a distant location, so their price must cover transportation expenses. What is needed is a locally available neighborhood service, to keep both you and your customers' costs down.

If you offered a local "vacation service" and advertised it by door-to-door flyer, you could start a lucrative business that requires very little time, expense or materials. Give your prospective customers a very specific list of what you will provide for what price. The list should include a disclaimer, a statement disavowing legal responsibility should theft or property damage occur while customers are away. This disclaimer will make some customers nervous. The best way to counteract the negative impact of such a disclaimer is to have a good list of references handy. If you have little or no business experience, a good character reference from a teacher or pastor will do.

To offer an attractive price, check the competition. You should be able to offer service in your own neighborhood for half the competition's price and still earn good wages. Offer two to three different levels of service at different prices. Some homeowners may even want you to sleep in their home while they are away. If so, charge a premium for overnight stays (with your parents' permission, of course).

One method of advertising is the door-to-door flyer. However, keep in mind that people don't need this service very often and may read your flyer and forget about you long before their vacation rolls around. You'll have to be inventive to keep your name on everyone's mind. Post notices everywhere; consider putting ads in the newspapers. Also, you might build up a larger clientele by advertising to local businesses. Real estate agents are often responsible for looking after and keeping up a number of vacant houses. Contact them directly and offer a quantity discount for their business. Having just one real estate agent for a customer could get you all the business you need. Also, contact personnel directors of local businesses. Often, they are responsible for looking after houses for employees who are relocating, or are away on extended business trips. Banks are another source of potential revenue. Many times bankers get stuck with empty houses when people stop paying their mortgages to the bank and move out. The house then becomes the property of the bank, which can't afford to let empty but valuable homes get run down or vandalized.

Idea

Party Helpers

Job Description: Caterer

Personal Traits Required: A talent for food preparation and creative flair

Experience Required: Depends upon service provided. For simple party assistance, no experience is required.

Materials Required: None for basic party helper service

Supplemental Materials Required: Party recipes & ingredients, decorations, invitations

Marketing Method: Flyers, newspaper ads, direct contact with local caterers and gourmet shops

Expected Wages: $5 per hour

Most people certainly can't afford household help, but at party time, everybody could use an extra set of helping hands. There are companies in larger cities that furnish maids, servers or chefs for a party, but they charge at least $12 per hour to cover the cost of their overhead, transportation and labor.

You could offer a party service, which could include some or all of the following:

▶ helping the host or hostess get ready, including food preparation, table or buffet setting, party decorating and light cleaning

▶ services during the party, such as filling hors d'oeuvres trays, punch bowls, etc.

▶ cleanup during and after the party

▶ serving courses during a dinner party

The key to success will be your professional approach. Read all you can on entertaining, from food preparation to decorating to party games. Be ready to offer suggestions to your prospective host or hostess.

The fee you charge should depend on the type of service you offer. For a simple party helper who takes directions from the host or hostess, charge $4 to $6 per hour. Or, if you have some good experience, talent and a knack for organizing, you could graduate into the big leagues and become a full-fledged "Party Planner." These are pros who plan and prepare every phase of a party, from issuing invitations to decorations to food to cleanup. They offer complete parties at a set fee per person to cover everything. Many offer packaged "theme parties," with standard food and decorations, such as a Fifties party, safari party, circus party, etc. The only limits are your imagination and abilities. To be a successful, full-fledged party planner, practice first on being a basic party helper to get some experience.

There are a few things to watch out for. You can't serve or handle alcoholic drinks in most states legally until you are twenty-one, so your customer must be aware you cannot tend bar, buy or serve liquor to guests. If you are going to offer assistance with food preparation, you must know your way around a kitchen before you sell that service to others.

If you want to get serious about such a service, you might also want to offer your own special hors d'oeuvres or party food. You could specialize in such things as meat and cheese trays, or hot canapes. If so, practice using these recipes before you sell them. See what the competition is offering. Many grocery stores offer party trays. First, find out if you can offer the same thing at a lower price, and still earn at least $4 to $5 an hour for your labor; otherwise, the extra effort won't be worth your time.

This service will probably be successful only in a large, well-to-do urban or suburban community whose residents do a lot of entertaining. You may find that there's not enough demand for this service in your immediate neighborhood. You could start advertising with a door-to-door flyer, but if you can't find enough customers, try advertising in the local newspaper. Another marketing tactic would be speaking directly to local caterers to see if they could use extra hands. Also, you could advertise by putting up posters where people buy party food.

Idea

Window Washing

Job Description: Window washer

Personal Traits Required: Upper body strength, patience and attention to detail

Experience Required: Washing a few windows first

Materials Required: A bucket, rags or newspapers or window washing blade, ammonia or other glass cleaning solution, perhaps a ladder

Marketing Method: Door-to-door flyer

Expected Wages: $5 to $8 per hour

If you have a strong arm, a desire to work hard and earn money, and want to provide a necessary service for your neighbors, try window washing! Most of the professional window washing services are geared toward commercial buildings, and their pricing reflects this. Current rates for window washing in many urban areas start at $40 to $50 for the exterior only of a small, three-bedroom one-story home. A pro can do a job that size in about three hours. If you can match that speed and do a good job of cleaning, you could charge half the professional fee and earn well over $5 per hour. The cost of supplies is minimal: a bucket, ammonia, a window washing blade and rags or newspapers. If you have customers with second-story windows and you don't have transportation, they'll need to furnish you with a ladder.

Window washing is more difficult than many people think. Anyone can wash windows, but it takes a lot of practice to produce streak-free and sparkling windows. You need strong arm and shoulder muscles to apply enough pressure to clean a houseful of windows thoroughly. Don't be too ambitious at first—your muscles must get used to it. The pros use only one type of solution to clean windows: ammonia in a bucket of water. Most glass cleaners on the market today have a tendency to leave a soapy film that can be difficult to wipe off. Test several methods of cleaning to find the one that works best for you. For exterior windows, you might start by hosing down the windows to loosen the dirt.

There are three basic cleaning methods:

1. Use a large, rubber-bladed window washing tool on a wooden handle.

2. Use large cloth or lint-free paper rags. Don't buy them at the grocery; go to a janitorial supply store and buy supplies in bulk.

3. Use ordinary newspapers. Strange as it may seem, the newsprint can be amazingly effective in making glass sparkle.

Exercise caution when washing interior windows. Using a large amount of water and a blade on the inside of a home can cause problems. Too much dripping can damage or ruin woodwork and floors. The best method for interior washing is probably a spray bottle with ammonia solution and rags. Be wary of window washing gadgets marketed through mail-order catalogs. Most of them get some dirt off, but not enough for a professional job. Also, they aren't heavy duty enough for regular use.

Practice on a few homes first before you start charging money. Try all three methods to see what works best for you. The trick will be timing. Figure out how long it takes you to do an average house, so you can accurately estimate prices on your customers' homes. All houses are different, and prices for window washing vary. Some professionals quote by the number of windows. Some quote by the square footage of the house. For example, you could price homes under 2000 square feet at $20, homes over 2000 feet at $25 and up. Second-story windows will be much more time consuming. You should charge an additional flat fee for second-story work requiring a ladder.

If you become quite good at washing windows, consider expanding into commercial work. If you have transportation, or have commercial buildings in your neighborhood, offer your services to small businesses, schools and institutions.

Idea

House Cleaning

Job Description: Professional house cleaner

Personal Traits Required: Above average level of stamina, plus a passion for cleanliness

Experience Required: Some practice cleaning a house

Materials Required: Can be furnished by your customers

Marketing Method: Door-to-door flyer

Expected Wages: At least $5 per hour

Pick this idea only if you are ready for hard work. Cleaning a whole house at one time is physically demanding. Doing it more than once a week requires strength and stamina. There is great demand for this service, and a great potential for you to make excellent wages, but it requires organization, energy and commitment.

To be really good at cleaning houses, you need a basic cleaning plan, so that you know exactly what to do every minute when you're in a client's house, and follow an exact order of cleaning every time. Casual dusting and vacuuming in your own home doesn't adequately prepare you for this. You need to practice cleaning an entire house in one fell swoop, several times, before you can consider cleaning houses for money. Every cleaning activity should be timed so you know how long it takes. Then, have your mother or another adult critique your work. People won't pay you to clean their homes unless you can do it as well or better than they can.

There are two basic types of cleaning activities, wet work and dry work. Wet work includes scrubbing all the surfaces and floors in the kitchen, bathrooms and non-carpeted areas. Dry work is vacuuming and dusting. Most professional services limit their cleaning to those two basic types. Other cleaning tasks, such as those listed below, are extremely time-consuming, so the pros avoid them or charge extra for them. The following are some particularly troublesome cleaning tasks, which you may want to avoid as part of your regular service:

▶ Oven cleaning

▶ Refrigerator cleaning

▶ Interior window washing

▶ Waxing or oiling wood furniture

▶ Cleaning the fireplace

▶ Dusting mini-blinds

▶ Cleaning overhead light fixtures

▶ Vacuuming upholstery or curtains

▶ Washing baseboards

▶ Doing laundry and/or ironing

▶ Washing dishes

▶ Cleaning and/or washing knick knacks and knick knack shelves

▶ Making beds

▶ Cleaning wet bars

If you include these services in your basic cleaning package, you could end up making less than $1 per hour!

If you provide just the basic wet and dry service, it should take you three to four hours to clean the average 2,000 square foot house with 2 or 2 and ½ bathrooms. Professional services charge from $35 to $70 per week for that size house. You could price your service at $15 to $20, and easily be able to clean one house in one or two afternoons after school. Charge more for larger homes with more bathrooms. Bathroom cleaning is one task that really adds to your cleaning time.

A typical cleaning schedule might be this:

1. Kitchen

▶ Wipe down kitchen surfaces, including table and counter tops, and the exterior of the stove, refrigerator and microwave

▶ Scour sink

▶ Sweep floor

▶ Mop floor

2. Bathrooms

▶ Apply toilet bowl cleaner

▶ Scrub tub/shower

▶ Scour sink and sinktop

▶ Clean mirror

▶ Scrub toilet

▶ Mop floor

3. Dust entire house

4. Vacuum entire house

If you're serious about this business, find a book on cleaning techniques at your bookstore or library. It's impossible to list here all the techniques and products you should be familiar with. When pricing your service, charge at least enough to pay yourself $5 per hour, because it is hard work. The trick to making good money at this is being highly efficient. Do a good job, but spend the shortest possible time in the house. You have to keep your nose to the grindstone, and not let up until you are finished. Ask your customer to buy your cleaning products, and keep them organized in one central place. Make recommendations if you know of superior products you prefer to use.

Customers are usually very concerned about security problems and theft when letting someone in to their house while they are away. Provide good work references or at least solid character references from someone they will trust—a teacher, a minister, a respected business leader, etc. The fact that you are a neighbor should calm some of their fears. Ask for your own key, and treat it like gold. It's not a good idea for your clients to leave a key sitting around the outside of the house for you to use. If you can find it, so can a thief. When working, build up clients' trust by putting any small change, money or valuables you might find in a central location. If you break something, *don't* hide it! Write a note of apology and leave it where the customer can find it immediately.

If you have large blocks of time available, such as all day on Saturday, you could offer a special "Spring Cleaning" service. Besides all the basic wet and dry work, spring cleaning could tackle that long list of particularly troublesome cleaning tasks. Professional cleaning companies charge anywhere from $60 to $100 for a complete and thorough cleaning. It's very hard work; you should charge at least $40 for such a major cleaning project.

The demand for a good, reliable and reasonably priced cleaning service is very high. You shouldn't have trouble finding enough customers to make excellent weekly wages; just two or three weekly customers will provide you with excellent earnings. Neighborhood advertising with door-to-door flyers should bring you the few customers you need.

Before you begin service with a new customer, take time to do a thorough interview. Explain exactly what you offer, and at what price. If a customer insists on special cleaning tasks outside your normal cleaning service, either charge extra or drop one of your regular cleaning duties from your list. Walk through the house with the client, so you know your way round. Ask if he or she is particularly fussy about any cleaning task. Check what cleaning products clients prefer. Find out if any rooms or any valuables are off limits to you. Don't hesitate to discuss cleaning matters with your clients—it will give them confidence that you really know what you're doing.

Idea

22

Birthday Party Service

Job Description: Children's party planner

Personal Traits Required: Outgoing, love children

Experience Required: Working with small children would be a plus

Materials Required: Invitations, decorations, party favors, hats, whistles, tooters, candles, cake, punch, candy, games

Marketing Method: Door-to-door flyers, posters

Expected Wages: $4 to $6 per hour

This is a perfect service to offer to busy working parents, and it will be fun for you, too. You can organize and run children's birthday parties, from the invitations to decorations to food to entertainment. Many parents resort to holding birthday parties at the local "Hamburger Heaven" simply because they don't have time to do it themselves.

To make money in this business, you must do it right. The true test is whether or not the children really enjoy it. You can't get a good clientele going unless the neighborhood children start asking for you.

Gear parties to the ages of the children. For example, children under the age of four don't respond well to organized games like "pin the tail on the donkey." They just want to run around and play. Check with your local book store or library; they carry books about children's parties. Experience should also teach you what kids like at what ages.

A good party service should include:

▶ fun invitations (have parents give you the invitation list)

▶ cake, ice cream and candy (Check parents' and children's preferences. Some parents object to too many sweets; some children will eat only chocolate cake.)

▶ party favors

▶ hats, balloons and decorations

▶ party plates, cups and napkins. To hold down costs, buy heavy-duty plastic or ceramic dishes that you can re-use, decorate your own plain white paper goods, or try to locate a wholesaler that will sell directly to you.

▶ organized games and prizes

▶ entertainment

The most difficult item on this list will be preparing a birthday cake. Find one or two simple cake designs that you can decorate different ways, and use them over and over. You could buy a cake form such as a teddy bear or doll that's easy to decorate, rather than making layer cakes that require extensive and difficult frosting decoration. An alternative would be to arrange with a local bakery to sell you cakes at a discount, providing you order several from them. The centerpiece of any children's birthday party is the cake, so you can't do an amateur baking job if you want your business to grow.

Try to locate a party supplies wholesaler or at least buy in bulk at a discount house to save money on balloons, favors and decorations. The price for your birthday party service should be based on your costs. Determine the minimum cost you will incur for a professional job. Then, add at least $4 per hour for your own labor, which should include time for purchasing supplies, making the cake, setting up and attending the party, and cleaning up afterward. Your final price should compare favorably to what is available for parties at the local fast food restaurants, or parents won't buy it.

You can expand your business by offering other types of children's parties. There are always extra opportunities for making money around the holidays by offering special theme parties for children. Halloween is a perfect time to advertise parties for the little spooks and goblins in your neighborhood. Parties for Valentine's Day and Thanksgiving are also popular. After you have some experience, check with local day care centers. They may be willing to buy special occasion parties from you if your service is reasonably priced, and if you convince them you can do a good job. Having a long list of good references is the best way to sell to commercial day care centers.

The advertising technique you select will be based upon demand in your area. You may have enough business in your immediate neighborhood. If so, the door-to-door flyer would be a good advertising method. The flyer should be colorful and appeal to parents and children as well. Post colorful notices on all local community bulletin boards: the library, rec center, school, church, synagogue. A particularly good place to advertise directly to your customers, working parents, is at day care centers. Call around your area and see if day care centers will allow you to pin up one of your posters or business cards in a prominent spot for advertising. If you don't have enough business in your neighborhood, and you have access to a car, you could serve a broader geographical area by putting an ad in your local newspaper.

Idea

23

Home Bakery

Job Description: Baker

Personal Traits Required: You must love to cook and have an outgoing personality to market your wares.

Experience Required: Depends upon product selected

Materials Required: Recipe ingredients, a reliable oven and stove, baking pans and utensils

Marketing Method: Direct sales

Expected Wages: $4 and up per hour

If you enjoy baking, and if you have reliable kitchen appliances and a good place to work at home, consider this business opportunity. In recent years, there has been a boom in consumption of gourmet baked goods. Witness the success of the expensive cookie stands in virtually every shopping mall in the country. The latest craze is muffin stalls, selling tasty fruit and nut muffins of every variety. During the 1960's and 1970's, baked goods and sweets disappeared, victims of the nation's obsession with diet and exercise. Now, pies, cakes, cookies, brownies, muffins and breads all seem to be experiencing a rebirth in popularity. To be successful in today's competitive baking environment, the goods must taste fresh, must use only the best ingredients, and must be distinctive.

If you want to get into the home baking business, the best bet is to specialize in JUST ONE THING. If you want your business to grow, your product must be better than the competition's. Some young entrepreneurs have taken their recipes for terrific cookies and turned them into nationwide, franchised businesses.

The first step is to select an excellent product, one that you can make with consistently good results over and over. That takes skill and practice. Use your friends and family as expert taste testers during this first, experimental phase of your business. Some of the ideas listed below don't require extensive experience or fancy equipment, such as muffins and cookies. However, the international desserts or cake decorating will take a lot of practice and perhaps a cooking class to product good results. Some product ideas:

1. Muffins, especially the type bursting with fruit and nuts. Gourmet bake shops, delis and frozen food sections of the grocery stores are just beginning to stock this newly popular item. The going rate per muffin is anywhere from $1 to $2. These aren't the dinky variety you whip up from a mix. At that price, the muffins must be large, contain the best ingredients, and be pleasing to the eye.

2. Cookies, the more exotic the better. As competition heats up in the cookie business, stores race to find new cookie recipes. Stores are now selling cookies containing macadamia nuts, fruit chips, gourmet chocolate cut in chunks rather than chips, coconut, and crushed candies. Shopping mall stores sell cookies at from 60 cents to $1.25 each.

3. Fancy cheesecakes New ideas for cheesecake flavors crop up every day as finishing touches to gourmet meals. Most exclusive restaurants serve elaborately decorated specialty cheesecakes. Delis and frozen food counters are also starting to carry the more expensive flavored cheesecakes.

4. Specialty breads People's taste for bread products is growing more diverse. No longer is soft, white bread the mainstay of American diets. Bread containing unusual grains, fruit, cheese, nuts, vegetables, herbs, spices and ethnic breads are now stocked in grocery stores. Trendy restaurants, even moderately priced establishments, compete to find unusual and tasty breads to serve with their main courses.

5. International desserts Interest is growing in international desserts such as Greek baklava, Mexican flan, German black forest cake, Viennese linzertorte, and English trifle. This might be a good choice if you have an old family recipe for an exquisite dessert, or can find and duplicate a good foreign recipe.

6. Cakes, particularly decorated birthday and wedding cakes. This can be a lucrative home business; however, you will have some startup costs for cake pans and decorating equipment. Also, you'll need to take a class and/or have extensive experience in decorating techniques.

Be sure to test your products extensively before you sell them. Determine the shelf life—how long your baked goods stay fresh and delicious—before you start marketing. Try freezing them, then thawing them to see if they retain their flavor and consistency. If your product freezes well, you can bake in advance in large quantities, then sell them as needed.

You'll need to price your baked goods high enough to cover ingredient costs plus your labor hours for baking and marketing. Also, if you sell to another outlet for final sale, such as restaurants or grocery stores, the price needs to be low enough so they can make money, too.

Example
Cora's Muffins

Cora decides to bake blueberry nut muffins to sell at school. After doing some test marketing at school, she determines she can sell six dozen per week by setting up a table after school every day for thirty minutes. It takes her two hours to bake and package six dozen muffins single in plastic wrap. She does her baking on Saturday for the following week. Cora wants to earn $4 per hour for her baking.

Labor for baking and wrapping	2 hours	
Labor for selling after school	2.5 hours	
Total labor hours	4.5 hours	
× Hourly Rate	$ 4	
Equals labor charge		$18
Ingredients–$2.50 per dozen × six dozen		15
Total cost for six dozen muffins		$33

$33 cost divided by 60 muffins = 55 cents per muffin

Cora decides to sell her muffins for 75 cents. At 55 cents, she will cover the cost of her ingredients and labor at $4 per hour. However, she decides to charge an additional twenty cents per muffin because the competition at the grocery store for fresh baked muffins charges $1.25, and the additional profits will help her buy additional muffin-baking equipment for future sales.

Example:
Tom's Cheesecake

Tom recently visited Pierre's, an exclusive restaurant, with his family. His favorite dessert is white chocolate cheesecake. He noticed Pierre doesn't offer cheesecake, but that other gourmet desserts on the menu were selling from $2 to $3.50. Tom's specialty is cheesecake, so he gets the brilliant idea of selling to Pierre. (Many fine restaurants buy pre-made desserts from outside vendors.) Restaurants try to keep their food costs to thirty percent or less of the final price to the customer, to cover overhead costs. Tom knows he can get twelve slices out of a cheesecake, and that the restaurant can sell the dessert for $2.50 per slice, or $30 for the whole cake. Tom knows the ingredients for one of his fine cheesecakes cost $5, and it takes him one hour to make one. If he can sell a cake to Pierre for $10, Tom will have covered his costs, earned $5 per hour for baking, plus kept under the restaurant's thirty percent guideline for food costs. He bakes a sample, decorates it beautifully, and takes it to the restaurant for the owner to try. Pierre promptly places a standing order for five per week! That's great news, because Tom can bake and decorate five in three hours. His estimates his profits to be:

Selling price for 5 cheesecakes	=	$50
Ingredients for 5 cakes @ $5 each	=	25
Profit for five cheesecakes		$25

$25 divided by three hours labor = $8.33 per hour

Based upon these profit projections, Tom immediately begins expansion plans to market to other fine restaurants in the area.

You'll need to be creative about marketing your products. Here are some marketing outlets you might consider:

1. At school This is probably the easiest outlet for sales. If you want to sell at school, keep to the simpler, less expensive baked goods, such as cookies, brownies or muffins. You can sell after lunch or after school. Hang out close to the cafeteria or set up a regular location on the school grounds.

2. Restaurants If you sell fancy, decorated desserts or unusual breads you can market to upscale restaurants in your area. Remember, you'll need to price your goods at thirty percent or less of the final price to the restaurant customer, so the owner can make money. Check prices on restaurant menus before setting your price.

3. Caterers Contact local caterers. They rarely make everything they sell to their clients. If you make an outstanding product, particularly one that would be served at parties, this would probably be a good opportunity for you.

4. Door to door If you live in a large, affluent neighborhood, try marketing with a door-to-door flyer, particularly around the holiday season. You'll need an attractive photo and/or delicious description to sell your wares.

5. Local grocery stores Visit the manager at the local grocery store. Be SURE to take samples. Suggest that your gourmet baked goods be carried in the delicatessen, gourmet section or frozen food counter.

6. Retirement or nursing homes Check with local homes to see if they might buy baked goods. They may be good outlets for selling healthy, high-fiber breads and muffins—or birthday cakes for residents.

One word of caution about the home bakery business. In some cities, baking in the home is against zoning or health ordinances. Check with the local officials before you start operation.

School-based Ventures

24. Buttoneer
25. Alternative Newspaper
26. Bumper Stickers
27. Typing Service
28. T-Shirts
29. Promoting the School Colors
30. Special Product Service

The ideas in the last two sections are primarily neighborhood businesses, with adults as your target market. As a student, you have a real opportunity to address a captive market right at your own school. You have access to your fellow students five days a week, so selling should be easier.

Your keys to success in selling at school are uniqueness and timing. First, find a product or service that no one else is offering. This section contains just a few suggestions; countless others could start you on your road to riches. Second, pay careful attention to timing. If you want to sell buttons or bumper stickers supporting one of your athletic teams, you must have them prepared well before the big game. Also, be aware of the natural life of your product. Students always want something new and different. You can't expect to sell the same old T-shirt all year long. Always be thinking ahead toward launching the next big product.

One word of caution about the ideas in this section. Unlike the business ideas in the first two sections, most of the ideas here involve selling products at retail—selling directly to the public. In most states, you must collect and pay state sales tax on retail products. See Chapter 3 for details on how to apply for a sales tax permit. Some states don't collect sales tax on income from service businesses. For example, Idea #27, Typing Service, doesn't involve selling retail products, just your labor and expertise. Laws and applications differ from state to state, so check with your local authorities.

Although this section is called "School-based Ventures," most of the ideas can be applied outside school as well. Marketing ideas for outside sales are explored in each section. Good luck!

Idea

24

Buttoneer

Job Description: Retail salesperson

Personal Traits Required: Artistically inclined

Experience Required: Calligraphy or layout experience would be necessary for some, but not all, types of buttons

Materials Required: Button-making machine and supplies

Marketing Method: Posters, direct selling, classified ads

Expected Wages: Unlimited potential

Teenagers love to wear buttons or badges proclaiming everything from their political convictions to support for the school team to the name of their current love interest. A button-making machine is relatively inexpensive to buy, and buttons can be made for a few pennies each. You can set your own price, and you probably won't have any local competition. The going rate for buttons is in the $1 to $5 dollar range.

Buttons are easy to make. You have only four parts to assemble: the button back, the pin insert, the artwork or printing itself, and a plastic or acrylic overlay to protect the artwork. The buttons can be assembled by hand, but the results are much more professional if you purchase an inexpensive button press.

There are a variety of sources for purchasing the equipment. Check at your library, in the back of magazines geared to small businesses or entrepreneurs. Or, talk to local printers. They may know some good sources. One nationally advertised company is:

>Badge-A-Minit
>348 North 30th Road
>LaSalle, IL 61301
>Phone (815) 224-2090

For $29.95, they will send you a starter kit, which includes a button or badge press and enough material to make 10 buttons. They also offer a free catalog of button-making products and ideas. Before you place an order, check with them for current price and delivery information. Shop around your area—you may find a local supplier of button-making equipment for less money.

There are literally thousands of ideas you can use for making buttons. The most popular buttons for school are those supporting athletic teams and events. Slogans for each game, such as "BEAT BEANTOWN" could be printed in advance and sold at school, at pep rallies, and in the parking lot before the game. Besides marketing at school and at games, you could sell buttons to local merchants in large quantities for them to sell. Get a copy of the school calendar, so you can print buttons way in advance for the entire school year, promoting all the school events. Try making a big sale to your student council or other student organization for one of their projects or fund-raisers. Buttons could also be promoted during student elections. Speak with the candidates at the very beginning of their campaigns to assure timely delivery.

Personalized buttons are in great demand. A popular idea these days is to laminate small photographs, usually of a current boyfriend or girlfriend, onto buttons. This type of button doesn't require any artistic talent or printing expense. Happy Birthday So-And-So buttons could also be bestsellers.

You can choose to hand-draw all your button art, if you have artistic talent. Or, you can draw up a sketch and have a local printer print it in sizes to fit your buttons. This method is expensive, so reserve it for buttons you plan to sell in large quantities. You can simply hand-letter a button slogan, and photocopy the slogan. This is an extremely cheap way to produce a large quantity. Or, instead of hand-lettering, you can use a computer graphics program or the rub-off letters found at art or office supply stores to generate the original slogan, then photocopy as many as you need.

Another method of producing buttons is to let a professional company do the work for you. Check the yellow pages under *Advertising Specialties* for a local button manufacturer. The advantage to this method is that all you must supply is a basic sketch of the button you want. If you take a copy of your school logo (the printer's word for an artistic symbol) or mascot, the manufacturer can reproduce it on a button. They do all the printing and assembly work. Also, this method probably produces the best-looking product. The disadvantages are that the buttons will cost you more than preparing them yourself, and you must order in large quantities, at least one hundred at a time. The price per button will depend upon the quantity you order, button size, number of colors and type of artwork you want. A typical price quote from a manufacturer should be something like this:

Button type: 2½ inch, white background with one color lettering and a logo

Minimum Order Quantity: Usually 100 buttons

Typical Price Quote:

For 100 buttons	$100, or $1.00 per button
For 250 buttons	$150, or 60 cents each
For 500 buttons	$200, or 40 cents each
For 1,000 buttons	$300, or 30 cents each

Add to the button charges a one-time only art layout fee in the neighborhood of $15. If you want more than one color for the lettering or logo, add about $15 extra per color.

Expand your sales outside of school by contacting local organizations for booster badges. Offer to print buttons for them in quantity to promote local events such as fairs, community awareness campaigns, charity fund-raisers, etc. Also, think of unique buttons that you could market to specialty stores. "I'm a new grandma" or "I'm a big brother" would sell well to baby boutiques, if your button is designed and printed in a professional manner. "World's greatest cook" or similar slogans would sell at cookware and gourmet shops.

When your business really takes off, develop some catchy, original slogans and consider expanding your marketing beyond your school and community. Try placing a few ads in regional or national newspapers. Think of how popular such catchphrases as "Where's the beef?" or "You look mah-velous!" or even the old "smiley face–have a nice day" have become nationwide. Don't rip off other people's work, though. You could get hit with a lawsuit. One great advantage of the badge/button business is that it's been around for well over a hundred years, and never seems to go out of style!

Idea
25

Alternative Newspaper

Job Description: Editor and journalist

Personal Traits Required: Writing aptitude and organizational skills

Experience Required: Basic typing

Materials Required: Typewriter or word processor, access to printer or ditto machine, paper

Marketing Technique: Various. See text.

Expected Wages: Unlimited potential

Here is a fun and entertaining idea for someone with superior organizational skills. Every school has a newspaper, but does it contain everything students want? The answer is usually *no*. In most schools, there's a real alternative to make money with an alternative newspaper. As long as the news you print isn't libelous (making unfavorable statements about persons or organizations without proof or justification) or vulgar (using obscene, gross or offensive language), your school authorities should allow you to distribute another paper. Schedule an appointment with the principal to discuss it, and have a sample ready. You don't want the school to shut you down after you've spent a lot of time and money. If the authorities don't want to cooperate, you are still within your legal rights to produce a newspaper, but you won't be able to advertise or distribute it on school property.

What do your fellow students want to read about that's missing from your school paper? The best way to find out is to take a casual poll among your friends. Here are just a few suggestions:

▶ interviews on hot topics
▶ advice to the lovelorn
▶ dating service
▶ sports coverage
▶ jokes and humor
▶ poetry
▶ gossip (be careful to avoid libel)
▶ comments & criticism of school activities and events
▶ music news and events
▶ community services geared to youth
▶ advertising, especially for other student-run businesses
▶ cartoons

The possibilities are endless. The best place to start is to check your own school newspaper to see what's missing.

The cost to produce a newspaper will fluctuate a great deal depending upon what method you use to produce the paper, labor expense, local printing costs, and what free resources you might be able to tap. Four basic production techniques are open to you:

1. Computer generation Several easy to use and inexpensive (in the $35 to $70 range) software packages are now available for producing small newspapers on personal computers. One example of a reliable, inexpensive software package is called Newsroom. It sells for less than $50 and is available for IBM and Apple personal computers. Most software packages will generate neatly formatted text and headlines, and will also produce graphics you can use for cartoons, decorations and borders. Besides the software, you will need a personal computer with two disk drives or a hard disk, plus a printer. If you have access to a computer, your production costs will include the price of the software plus about two cents per page to cover the paper and ribbons. Your printer generates the copies, so you won't have any reproduction costs. Computer production is by far the fastest and easiest production method. If you don't have a computer, many local libraries will allow you to use or rent one on their premises. Also, check with your school to see if you could use theirs. If you don't have access to a computer, don't run out and buy a big system! Use one of the other methods listed below, at least until you have some proven revenue.

2. Stencil/ditto machine Many schools and churches have ditto machines you might be allowed to use. This method uses a master copy generated on a typewriter using special stencil paper. This stencil master can print hundreds of copies on a ditto machine. Your only out-of-pocket expenses are for the stencil master and paper; usually less than one cent per page. The major drawback to this method is that you must be a very accurate typist—it's difficult to correct typing mistakes on stencils. Plus, you cannot generate any graphics, borders or large print headlines.

3. Typewriter/graphics/copy machine You can generate a very nice-looking newspaper using an ordinary typewriter, especially if you enhance the copy with graphics and/or hand-drawn cartoons. You can find large and decorative rub-on or paste-on letters for headlines at any office supply store. Photocopy charges will run you from three to twenty cents per page, depending upon your community.

4. Typeset/offset printing If you are going to produce your newspaper in large quantities, it may be more economical to have your paper professionally printed. Check with your local printer to compare printing versus photocopy costs. If you are going to have your paper printed using an offset press (the printer will explain this process to you), you must provide your printer with a perfectly typed copy. Many printers can take computer-generated material from your diskette and print directly from it, thereby saving you the typesetting fees. The printer can enhance the looks of your newspaper by adding borders, graphics and extra-large letters for headlines. Price will depend on the quantity and quality of the paper and ink used. Offset printing will give you the most professional results, but will be too expensive in small quantities.

The best way to finance the newspaper is to sell advertising. Invite students to use your display or classified ads, a great marketplace for student-oriented products and services (your fellow entrepreneurs!). This would be an ideal place for personal messages to friends or loved ones. You could even offer a "cupid column." With enough advertising revenue, you could distribute your newspaper free. Another source to tap for advertising revenue would be local businesses who want to reach the student market. Good businesses to check with would be local teen clothing stores, record shops and restaurants close to school. Mention coupons as a good promotional tool to include in their ads. Also, check local fast food restaurants. They always seem to be short of help. Your newspaper would be the perfect place for them to place a "help wanted" ad. You could send them information and rates via a short letter in the mail, by telephone, or schedule a short visit.

You'll need to do some detailed planning to determine costs and a selling price, but the example on the following page should give you some ideas.

Your newspaper's success will depend on skillful marketing and distribution. Build up curiosity about your paper before publication! Here are some methods you could try:

▶ posters & banners

▶ "giveaways" such as balloons printed with the paper's name

▶ stage a get-together for influential student leaders at your house to announce publication

▶ announcements over the school loudspeaker

▶ signs on or near the school grounds

▶ flyers on cars in the parking lot

▶ contests for best story, best poem, etc.

▶ offer a fun prize – include an entry form in the first edition

Example

Business Plan for the *Beagleville Growl* Newspaper

Cost estimate (for one edition):

(Based upon your labor at $5 per hour)

Writing time, gathering and writing up the news:	30 hrs.
Typing time:	10
Distribution/advertising:	10
Total labor hours	**50**

50 hours @ $5 per hour =	$250

Estimated total distribution: 500 copies

Estimated pages per copy: 10 pages

Total pages: 500 copies × 10 pages per copy = 5,000 pages

Printing costs:

Photocopy charges 5,000 sheets × 5 cents per page

$250

(Printing costs vary depending
upon printing method chosen)

Total costs per edition	**$500**

Now, if you can sell $500 worth of advertising, you could distribute the paper free and still earn a minimum of $5 per hour. Or, the students may feel they are getting something worth having if you charge a small fee, 50 cents for example. That is a management decision for you to make. Here's an example of estimating revenue, based upon selling classified ads to students at $3, 1 inch display ads to local businesses for $20 (see information about display advertising in Chapter 5), and selling the newspaper to students for 50 cents:

Revenue estimates:

300 copies @ 50 cents	$150
(If you charge, not all students will buy)	
40 student classified ads @ $3 each	120
12 business display ads @ $20 each	240
Total estimated revenue	**$510**

Besides the big decisions about what you will print, what it will cost and the price, another big business decision will be your method of distribution—how to get your paper out to the students. This will depend somewhat upon whether or not you're charging your readers. If the paper is free, you can simply leave copies in stacks somewhere on the school grounds, with large posters or banners calling attention to them. Or, you could stick the papers through locker slots or leave them on car windows. If you will charge, then you'll need a central location where you can sell papers and collect money. This might take coordination with school officials.

The newspaper business is hard work, but it is also fun and professionally rewarding, particularly if you plan to make a career in journalism. The experience will make an outstanding entry on a college application or resume.

Idea

26

Bumper Stickers

Job Description: Slogan artist

Personal Traits Required: Outgoing personality for marketing

Experience Required: None

Materials Required: Bumper sticker paper and weatherproof paints, or contact a local printer

Marketing Method: Posters, direct sales

Expected Wages: Unlimited potential

The business of bumper stickers is basically the same as Idea #24, Buttoneer. This is a venture where you develop catchy slogans or artwork, only your artistic canvas is the bumper sticker, rather than the button.

Professional bumper sticker manufacturers make the stickers in four sizes, ranging from 3 inches by 7½ inches to 3¾ inches by 15 inches. You can make them yourself, or contact a local supplier to print them for you.

If you manufacture your own stickers, you'll need to buy gummed paper and weatherproof paint. Contact a local paper supplier for the gummed paper, which has a peel-off backing. You can't paint bumper stickers with ordinary paint or magic markets; the paint will bleed or fade in a few days. Purchase paint especially designed to withstand the weather.

Before you sell your own design, test your paint by drawing up a few stickers and leaving them outside for at least a week. Spray them with water to make sure they are colorfast.

Lately, another option for bumper sticker manufacture has appeared in national advertisements. You can buy a device to print your own stickers at home. Check the classified sections of major newspapers or hobbyist magazines such as *Popular Mechanics* for details. The great advantage of having your own printer is convenience. However, these home devices don't give you options as to color, artwork or size.

The best bet for making professional-looking stickers is to have a local supplier print them for you. The price will depend upon the size, the artwork, the quantity and number of colors you choose. A typical price quote should look like this:

Bumper sticker: White background with simple logo and one color lettering

Size: 3¾ × 7½ inches

Minimum Order Quantity: Usually 125

Typical Price Quote:

125 stickers	$130, or $1.04 each
250 stickers	$150, or 60 cents each
500 stickers	$200, or 40 cents each
1,000 stickers	$250, or 25 cents each

Add to these prices $20 to $50 if you use a logo or other artwork, to cover the layout fee. If you want more than one color for the logo or lettering, add about $15 per order per extra color.

Your local printer may do bumper stickers, but the best bet is to contact an advertising promotion firm. They print everything from mugs to shirts to hats to bumper stickers. Just as with the button idea, if you take your school logo or mascot to the company, they can reproduce it beautifully right on the sticker, for a one-time fee of about $20. They keep the artwork, so if you re-order, you won't have to pay any additional money for another logo.

Promote your product every chance you get at school. Paste your stickers on your locker, books, everywhere people might see them. Set up a table or booth outside athletic events if you have a sticker promoting the team. Parents will certainly want to buy team booster stickers. Offer your stickers at local drug and department stores, giving them a discount if they buy in quantity. If you think of a particularly catchy slogan that has universal appeal, consider advertising in local newspapers or regional magazines. Keep in mind you'll probably have to charge more to cover your advertising and postage expenses.

Idea
27

Typing Service

Job Description: Professional typist

Personal Traits Required: You must be a whiz in spelling, English and grammar. Also, good people skills are required. Customer relations is a critical element of this business.

Experience Required: Advanced typing skills—you should be able to type at least fifty words per minute with very few mistakes.

Materials Required: Electric typewriter, paper, ribbons

Marketing Method: Posters, classified ads

Expected Wages: $5 to $10 per hour

Typing is one of the best methods to earn regular, steady income from now through your golden years. You won't get rich, but there's always a demand for a quality typist. It's a great way to work yourself through college, because you can schedule your workload around your studies. The faster and more accurately you type, the more money you can earn. In the past, many people never bothered to learn how to type. However, a whole new attitude is developing now that fast typing skills are in demand in the world of computers.

Peggy Glenn, in *Word Processing Profits at Home,* states, "As a general rule, if you can produce a single page of double-spaced pica typing in ten minutes with only three or four errors, you can make money at it. . . . Timed typing speed of 65–80 words per minute with accuracy is the ideal starting point for self-employment." However, Ms. Glenn expects to earn $15 per hour for her typing. If you can produce high-quality typing at fifty words per minute, you'll still be able to earn a good wage.

What if your typing skills aren't that good? Because typing is such a great part-time business, making an investment in improving your skills will certainly pay off. Take a refresher course at your high school or local community center. Or, check a typing drill book out of the library and time yourself. Audio cassettes are now available that teach basic typing. You can even learn from a computer. Many community libraries now offer free computer time and learning programs. If you've never typed before, you can get up to speed in three to six months with diligent practice, and typing is a skill that will help you throughout your life.

What about equipment? Most professional typists use expensive word processing machines or personal computers. That's not necessary to type the average school paper. If you have a reliable electric or electronically enhanced typewriter, that's good enough. (A manual, non-electric typewriter is *out!* It produces very inconsistent type quality.) The price of high-quality typewriters has come down dramatically in the past few years. Certain new electronic models offer some of the same features as expensive word processing machines, such as automatic centering and spelling checkers, for less than $500. If your business takes off, you'll make enough to purchase the fancy equipment later. If you don't own a typewriter, and don't have enough cash for the purchase, consider leasing from an office supply store. Word processing machines *are* wonderful, but they don't greatly increase your speed for a one-time-only typing job. Their special magic comes in handy when you're generating numerous form letters or extensive document revisions.

Establishing your pricing policy will be difficult. Your primary market will be fellow students, so you will be typing fairly straightforward papers and reports. (Pricing gets tricky when you type difficult technical documents with formulas, columns of numbers or equations.) Professionals charge anywhere from $1 to $5 per double-spaced, non-technical page of type. Check your local competition, and try to undercut their prices. If you type slowly but accurately at fifty words per minute, and charged 80 cents per page, you should be able to generate six pages an hour after proofreading and making corrections. This would earn you $4.80 per hour. Your speed should improve dramatically if you type at least eight hours every week, so $4.80 will be your starting wage. As speed improves, your hourly wage will soar!

One of the problems with typing for a living is customer relations. Some of your customers will hand you barely readable, scribbled pages and expect you to turn them into a masterpiece. Lay down the law in the beginning about the quality of the manuscripts you type from, and charge extra for poor-quality drafts to protect yourself. For example, charge $5 per hour for extra work to "decode" a document. This would include making phone calls to your customer to decipher unintelligible hieroglyphics, or extra time you spend to correct subhuman English that contains glaring grammar, construction or punctuation errors. One of the best ways to avoid problems is to sit down and read aloud through the document with your customer, side by side, before you start typing the document. Another way to avoid problems and misunderstandings is to charge one fee, say 80 cents per page, for "as-is" typing, typing exactly what your customer hands you, mistakes and all. Then, you could charge more, say $1.25, for edited typing, where you go the extra mile to clean up your customer's English mistakes. No matter how bad the paper is, the best policy is this: don't ever try to rewrite or rephrase other people's work. They alone are responsible for content. If you know a client well, perhaps you can discuss glaring errors in composition *before* you begin typing. However, students' grades are supposed to be reflections of *their* efforts, not yours.

Another question that will probably come up is—who pays for mistakes in the finished document? If you typed an error into a document that wasn't in the original manuscript, the best policy is to fix it for free. If the error was your customer's, perhaps a dropped sentence or illegible handwriting, then charge your standard page rate for correction.

Your best market will probably be schoolmates. Picking up and delivering documents is easy, and selling your service should be as simple as putting up a few posters and word-of-mouth advertising. Once you gain some experience and speed, consider other markets. Post notices at schools and colleges in your area. If you don't drive, ask your customers either to mail documents or to deliver them in person. Place classified ads in the local newspaper, or talk directly to businesses and churches in your area.

If you will be dealing with strangers, or even with friends, establish a cash-only policy. *Never* hand back a document until you are paid. Promises to pay are often forgotten after the work is done, and collection is a *big* hassle.

Idea

28

T-shirts

Job Description: Fabric artisan

Personal Traits Required: An artistic bent and a flair for design

Experience Required: Depends upon artistic medium

Materials Required: Plain T-shirts. Other materials will depend upon method you select. See text below.

Marketing Method: Posters, flyers, samples

Expected Wages: Unlimited potential

Everyone wears T-shirts. It's a clothing craze that won't disappear in the foreseeable future. And everyone seeks the new and different design that best expresses a mood, philosophy, love interest, or school loyalty.

The variations in colors, design and method of manufacturing are countless. New ways to produce T-shirts crop up all the time. If you are planning on selling a lot of T-shirts, you'll need to find a wholesale supplier from which to buy materials in bulk. The best way to find a good supplier is to snoop around a T-shirt shop in your area. Ask store owners, perhaps in a neighboring town, where they buy supplies. Or contact a Chamber of Commerce in a large city for names of wholesale suppliers. A good-quality plain cotton T-shirt costs anywhere from $1.50 to $3 wholesale, and at least twice that in retail stores. You'll have a tremendous price advantage if you buy your blank T-shirts wholesale. The disadvantage is that you'll have to buy shirts in large quantities, which requires some cash up front.

Listed below are some of the most popular methods you can use to produce T-shirts. Some don't require any artistic ability, but some, like silk-screening, take quite a bit of experience and skill.

1. Iron-on letters This is the cheapest and easiest method to produce T-shirts, but also the least professional-looking. You simply decide on a slogan and a pattern for placing letters on the shirt, and apply the letters carefully with a hot iron. This method would probably be adequate for school slogans. Use one school color for the shirt and the other color for the lettering. You could market these not only during school hours by wearing samples to class, but also at sporting events by setting up a booth or table outside the gym or stadium. This technique could also be used for catchy slogans or personalized shirts. Shirts wishing people happy birthday are always popular. If one of your school organizations wins an honor, sell T-shirts such as "#1 All-State Choir", or "We're Number 1!" with the name of the team or organization.

2. Computer graphics You can produce 8½ by 11 inch artwork with slogans using inexpensive computer software programs such as Printshop. Kits are available to turn these graphics into T-shirt transfers. The transfer kits are expensive, but they give you many more design possibilities. Check with your local computer supply store for details. Look for a price break on the kits by checking with a large mail-order computer supplies firm. Any personal computer magazine will have ads for hundreds of mail-order companies.

3. Hand painting Fabric painting is a hot new craze, particularly on the West Coast. As a fabric painter, you make individual works of art for each of your customers. Buy special fabric paints that can survive repeat washings. These can be found at large craft stores. The paint comes in many wild and crazy colors—the most popular are the glitter paints. This technique requires real artistic ability. Since each shirt is painted by hand, you'll have to charge more than for the other techniques described here. Develop three or more standard designs that can be painted in less than an hour.

4. Applique Applique T-shirts are also very popular now. In this technique, you cut a pattern out of cloth and sew it directly on the shirt. Many applique designs are a mix of fabric styles, textures and colors. If you do mix fabrics, make sure they all shrink at the same rate as the cotton T-shirt. Otherwise, they look terrible after the first washing. The best applique fabric for T-shirts is colorfast cotton of a similar weight to the T-shirt. Many applique designs are dressed up with buttons, bows, ric-rac, lace and fabric paint.

5. Silk-screening This technique provides a very professional look, but is difficult to do well. You need to have extensive experience with the silk-screening process. The library has books describing the silk-screen method, but it really takes experience that can only be acquired in an art class. Basically, you develop an original design and print it on a T-shirt by squeezing ink through a piece of silk that has been very tightly stretched on a wooden frame. The design must first be made into a stencil that fits directly on the silk. The stencil can be developed using one of four techniques: photo-stencil, hand-cut film, paper or glue. The techniques are too complicated to be described here in any detail. If you are a capable artist, this method can provide the most satisfying results, and you can use the stencil over and over again.

6. T-shirt resale You can produce great results by letting someone else do all the work. T-shirt or advertising promotion companies can produce shirts with high-quality artwork in large quantities. You provide the basic design, they do all the rest. The advantage is that you'll get a professional-looking shirt. The disadvantage is that the finished product will cost more than if you had produced the shirt yourself, plus you must buy in large quantities. Track down a supplier by looking in the yellow pages of the biggest city close to you, under *T-shirts*. This will give you a listing of all the wholesale and retail suppliers. Also, you can check for a supplier in a large city phone book under *Advertising Specialties* or *Advertising Promotions*. Prices should run about like this:

Shirt type: One color lettering silk-screened onto a white or pastel-colored shirt with a simple logo

Minimum Order Quantity: Usually two dozen; orders increase in one-dozen increments

Typical Price Quote:

24 shirts	$132, or $5.50 per shirt
48 shirts	$180, or $3.75 per shirt
96 shirts	$307, or $3.20 per shirt

Besides the shirt printing fee, you will be charged a one-time screen charge of about $20 for one color, $35 for two colors. The screens can be used again if you place another order.

The manufacturer can give you a mix of sizes and colors, as long as you order at least one dozen of each color per size. So, if you order 96, you could order 12 pink adult small, 48 adult light blue medium, 24 gray adult large, and 12 beige adult extra-large. T-shirt experts say that the best shirt colors for printing are gray, beige and white.

The profit potential for T-shirts is very high. People are willing to pay at least $10 for a unique, quality-made shirt. If it costs you less than $5 for materials and you sold just one shirt an hour, you'd make $5 per hour. If you sold in quantities at athletic events, you could easily make $100 a night and up.

To promote your product, be a walking advertisement. Wear your products at every opportunity. Be willing to sell the shirt off your back! Keep several sizes handy; you'll be surprised at how many you sell. If you have a school or team booster shirt and school spirit is high in your neighborhood, think about selling T-shirts door to door. Set up a sales table outside community events, games and meetings, or even after school. Keep a notebook handy to keep track of sales and be ready to take large, special orders.

Idea
29

Promoting the School Colors

Job Description: Design artist

Personal Traits Required: Some artistic design and an outgoing personality

Experience Required: For most of the ideas—none

Materials Required: Depends upon what you offer—pennants, balloons, mugs, glasses, pencils, pens, jackets, sweatshirts

Marketing Method: Personal selling, posters, classified ads

Expected Wages: Unlimited potential

If you have lots of school spirit that you want to pass on, think about setting up a school "booster" business. There are hundreds of products available that can be printed with your school name and logo. You can either do the artwork yourself, or contact a professional printer or advertising promotions firm. This business requires direct, personal selling, so you must have an outgoing personality.

If you order your goods from an advertising promotions firm, you don't necessarily have to have any start-up capital. For example, if you want to sell blast jackets with your school emblem on the back, you can take advance orders from students. Once you have received students' money, you can place an order with the advertising promotions company. The profit-making potential for this idea can be substantial. For example, you can purchase baseball-style jackets from an ad promotion firm for $13 to $20, depending upon the company and the quantity. Most retail stores sell them at around $35. So, if you sell just five jackets per week, you'll net at least $75!

Some of the ideas for products you can make or hire a professional firm to make for you are listed below:

Pencils	Shoestrings
Pens	Pennants
Bookcovers	Window stickers
Notebooks	Boxer shorts
Mugs	Underwear

Glasses
Mufflers (the cold weather variety, not the auto)
Mittens
Hats
Caps
Sweatshirts
Sweatpants
Polo shirts
Tennis shirts
Tennis racket covers
Tennis balls
Golf balls
Blast jackets
Matchbooks
Stadium blankets for football games
Coolers
Baby clothes
Socks
Toilet Seats
Towels
Toothbrushes
Can holders
Book bags
Duffel bags
Sun visors
Thermos bottles
Car coffee mugs
Stickers
Stationery
Salt and pepper shakers
Key chains
Decals
Tie tacks
Jewelry
Paperweights and desk accessories

All these products and countless more have been used as vehicles to display school pride. If you want additional ideas or want to see some samples, stroll through a large store that sells booster items in a big college town close to you.

The method you use to make booster items is up to you. There are too many on the list to give detailed instructions on manufacturing techniques. Some of the items are good candidates for home manufacture. Or, you can find a company to make any or all of them for you. Look in the Yellow Pages under *Advertising Specialties* or *Advertising Promotions.*

If you plan on offering a variety of products, develop a flyer and advertise door to door in your community. Set up a booth at athletic events to promote your products. Local businesses might be interested in buying booster items in large quantities. Advertise in the local newspaper, too. The market for these products will be more than just your classmates.

If you are ambitious, consider producing products for other schools in your area. If a particular product you sell is "hot" at your school, it will probably sell well at another school or campus. If the school is close, you can drive over. Or, contact a friend at that school to be your distributor.

Idea
30

Special Product Service

Job Description: Retail salesperson

Personal Traits Required: Outgoing personality, good sales technique

Experience Required: None

Materials Required: Depends upon products you select

Marketing Method: Direct sales, leaflets

Expected Wages: Unlimited potential

What products do your classmates buy all the time? What are they always running out of at school? If you have the answers, and have an outgoing personality, you can probably set up a business selling useful products to your friends at school.

The key to success will be the convenience of your products. Try to hit on just one or a few good products that have income potential throughout the school year, and promote your products hard. Soon, students will come to you to buy instead of making that extra trip to the grocery or drug store. If you want to earn good money, locate a supplier who will sell you products at a deep discount or at wholesale. Check local prices for the product you're selling. You don't need to offer prices drastically lower than retail stores. Students should be willing to pay full retail price or even a little more for the convenience of buying at school. Only if you find a really great discount deal from a supplier should you consider selling your products at bargain prices.

Some of the products that might sell well at school are:

Pens
Pencils
Notebooks
Paper
Blank tape cassettes
Snack food
Calculators
Bookcovers
Report binders
Gym or sports equipment
Discount tapes or records

Books
Typing supplies
Jewelry
Handicrafts
Musical instrument
 supplies—strings, rosin,
 reeds
Datebooks
Calendars
Organizers

Blank video tapes
VCR movies that class-
mates can rent and
return to you
Greeting cards
Cosmetics, such as Avon
or Mary Kay

Clothes—any hot and
trendy item
Hair accessories
Baked goods—brownies,
cookies, muffins
Personalized items of
every description

It's better to offer a few products and be a reliable supplier than try to be a full-service K-Mart. Keep on the good
side of school officials. Don't sell anything that's gross, offensive, illegal or immoral. Keep your prices consistent. Don't
offer discounts to friends. It will be impossible to keep accurate records if you offer different prices to different people. You can open your "store" at certain times, such as over
the lunch hour or right after school. Set up a regular place
to sell, so people know where to find you. You can put up
a booth or table on the school grounds, sell out of your locker
or the trunk of your car.

Ventures Using
Special Skills or Training

31. Clowning Around   **35.** Making Music

32. Giving Lessons   **36.** Bicycle Repair

33. Handicrafts   **37.** Telemarketing

34. Tutoring   **38.** Calligrapher

If you have a unique talent or skill, then capitalize on
it! One of the best methods for making money is selling what
you do best.

Three of the business ideas in this section can be learned
in a short amount of time with a little research and practice—
#31 Clowning Around, #36 Bicycle Repair and #37 Telemar-
keting. However, the other ideas require considerable expertise before you can turn them into a business.

Idea
31

Clowning Around

Job Description: Entertainer/actor

Personal Traits Required: An outgoing personality
and acting ability

Experience Required: Supplementary skills such as balloon artistry, juggling or magic

Materials Required: Clown suit: costume, wig, shoes, nose, makeup

Supplemental Materials Required: Balloons, magician's supplies, juggling supplies, horn, squirting flowers, etc.

Expected Wages: At least $10 an hour

If you are a real ham and love children, then you could be a clown! Being a good clown takes more than putting on a funny costume. You must be a combination of actor, artist, mime, comic, juggler and magician. Entertaining in public requires a great deal of self-confidence and poise. Above all, you must be willing to do silly things for laughs and enjoy every minute of it.

Clowning takes some initial investment. A complete clown outfit consists of a basic cotton costume, wig, goofy shoes, a makeup kit and perhaps a nose. You can enhance your costume with a squirting flower for your lapel or a large honking horn. The cost to purchase a complete, ready-made clown outfit should be in the range of $100 to $125. But you'll spend considerably less if you make the costume yourself. Most pattern catalogs contain a clown suit you can stitch up in several styles. You can also shop second-hand stores for such things as baggy pants and suspenders, wacky housedresses and wigs.

How do you pick up clowning skills? Some communities offer courses in clowning. A local magic shop might teach a course. A typical clowning class in a big city costs between $50 and $100, and should offer the basics of makeup, balloon animals, juggling and magic. Also, check with your librarian for one of the many books written about clowning.

There are three things you need to develop before you begin your business:

1. Clown face Many standard clown faces have developed over the years—some sad, some happy, some silly. Any book on clowning should have pictures you can use for your basic "face." Then add a few touches of your own. Develop a standard face for your clown "image," so you'll always look the same. Practice putting on your clown face with makeup in front of the mirror, until you can practically do it in your sleep.

2. Clown style Every clown needs to develop a "style"—a way of communicating with the audience. Some clowns are completely voiceless, communicating only with mime and facial expressions. Will you come across as a sad sack? Or be loud and silly? Children might respond better to a loud and raucous style punctuated with exaggerated gestures. Developing a style takes thoughtful consideration and practice until you're comfortable with it.

3. Clown routine Clowning takes more than showing up and smiling. You need a few tricks up your sleeve to entertain your audience. Most professional clowns are also balloon artists, jugglers, magicians, or all three. Children don't require sophisticated magic such as card tricks or "cut and restore" gimmicks. A few basic routines that surprise and delight them are all that's required, such as pulling flowers out of your sleeve, or coins from behind the kid's ears. It's a good idea to have little presents to leave with your audience, such as balloon animals. Making these animals takes practice. You'll also need special balloons, which you can obtain at magic stores, large toy stores or through mail-order catalogs.

Develop a standard thirty-minute show to use in your personal appearances. As soon as you have your routine down, practice with some little children. You must be able to get a lot of laughs. If not, you're doing something wrong. Ham it up, enjoy yourself! Kids can see right through you. If YOU aren't having a good time, they won't, either.

Clown work won't be as steady as some of the other business ideas in this book. You'll have to be very clever and persistent in marketing yourself to earn a good living. Because you will have to spend a lot of time selling, charge enough for a performance to cover your marketing time as well. Professional clowns in big cities charge between $40 to $60 for a short personal appearance, from thirty minutes to an hour. You should charge at least $15 to cover your labor plus additional expenses and transportation.

Here are some marketing tips to keep the work coming in:

▶ Drop off flyers in your neighborhood. Offer your services for birthday parties, hospital visits or family gatherings.

▶ Contact local businesses. Personal appearances by a clown in certain stores could be a big boost for business, particularly to draw in parents with small kids. This would be especially good for stores carrying children's products, such as clothing or toy stores. You won't necessarily have to go through a standard "routine" for these appearances. Just show up, talk to the children and hand out balloons.

▶ Contact local restaurants that cater to kids. The local fast food shop could really increase restaurant sales by having you around every Saturday. Also, if the restaurant offers a birthday party service, leave a business card or a flyer with the manager. He might suggest you as an entertainer for a party.

▶ Contact the local hospital's children's ward. Clowns can do a lot to cheer up sick children. See if the hospital will allow you to put up an advertising poster to remind parents.

▶ Put up posters where kids will see them—at grocery stores, day care centers, churches or community centers. Four-year-olds and up usually tell their parents exactly what they want for their birthday party. If you advertise where kids will see your poster, they'll ask for you.

▶ Make public appearances in costume in crowded places, such as shopping malls. Hand out business cards or flyers describing your services and fees. Who knows, you might earn a few tips!

Clowning takes a *lot* of bravado and self-confidence. You can build up your confidence, plus your business, by making all your sales calls and business contacts in costume.

Idea
32

Giving Lessons

Job Description: Teacher

Personal Traits Required: Patience and ability to communicate well

Experience Required: A high level of achievement in a skill someone will pay to learn from you

Materials Required: Usually none that you don't have already

Marketing Method: Door-to-door flyer, schoolboard notices, newspaper advertising

Expected Wages: At least $8 per hour

This is one of the few ideas in this book which does require an expert level of accomplishment in a field. Most of your competitors will be older; many will have college degrees in the field. Don't attempt to give lessons unless you are highly skilled. Otherwise, you will end up being frustrated, plagued with self-doubt and angry clients. However, you CAN compete successfully, particularly if you have had some recognition or experience in the field.

The advantages of teaching as a business are many. It's one business that can generate substantial, regular earnings year in and year out for the rest of your life. You don't *have* to have transportation; most lessons are given in teachers' homes. Plus you will have the satisfaction of utilizing your skills in an area in which you have already proven yourself.

The key to success in marketing your services will be a combination of low price and expertise. For example, the going rate for music lessons in most communities is $8 to $15 for a half hour of instruction. You could charge $4 per half hour, thus earning $8 an hour, and significantly undercut the competition. There are even greater earning possibilities in other areas. For example, computer classes in subjects like LOTUS 1-2-3 are priced at $200 to $400 per person per day! It would help if you had some professional credentials, such as contest awards, academic honors and/or prior teaching experience. Make sure you let your prospective clients know about these.

Some of the teaching areas currently in heavy demand are:

▶ Musical instruments

▶ Music theory

▶ Foreign languages

▶ Computer skills

▶ Baton twirling

▶ Makeup/beauty/fashion

▶ Programming

▶ Typing

▶ Shorthand

▶ Cooking

▶ Handicrafts–knitting, needlepoint, crochet, etc.

▶ Swimming

▶ Racquet sports– tennis, racquetball

▶ Word processing

▶ Preschool early learning–numbers, ABCs, phonics, reading

▶ Cheerleading

▶ Basic auto mechanics

▶ Baby-sitting skills

▶ Sports for kids–soccer, softball, basketball

▶ First aid and safety skills

These are just a few of the opportunities available. Some of the suggestions are primarily suited for private lessons. However, some of them–such as cooking, music theory, cheerleading and baby-sitting skills–are better taught in a group. You will have to charge less per client for group lessons, but these offer potential for greater hourly earnings.

Keep in mind that knowing how to do something well and teaching others how to do it are two separate skills. Your success as a teacher will depend upon adequate preparation. Develop a professional curriculum. Have each minute of the lesson planned in advance, so you don't waste your clients' time. Survey currently available teaching materials. Scan music or bookstores. Check with other teachers (check anonymously, as if you were interested in lessons from *them*. Don't tip off the competition!) to find out what materials they are using.

Keep your professional skills polished and keep current in the field. See if there are any professional publications you can subscribe to. There may be local clubs or associations you can join, such as a music teacher's group or a computer club. Your primary responsibility will be to keep well ahead of your students. Given your age and experience, gear your lessons to the beginner. You don't want someone showing up at your door with more experience than you.

Besides adequate preparation and polished accomplishment in your field, you'll need plenty of patience to teach beginners. As you gain experience teaching, you'll develop a sense about when to push your students and when to hold back. Whether you're giving group or private lessons, remember that no two students are alike. Try to recall what it was like for you to learn your skill, and apply your personal experience to teaching others.

You can probably drum up enough business in your own neighborhood to earn a good living. Try the door-to-door flyer method first. Stress your professional skills and qualifications in the ad, as well as your low price. State a target age group, say primary school beginners. Describe any advantages you offer which other teachers might not. For example, one advantage not offered by most teachers is providing lessons in the student's own home. Many parents would go for this; they get tired of carting their children around town for lessons and might enjoy hearing their little marvels acquire new skills right in their own living rooms. If you can't drum up enough business in the neighborhood, but have access to transportation, try advertising in the local newspaper.

Idea

33

Handicrafts

Job Description: Artist/Designer

Personal Traits Required: Artistic ability and outgoing personality for marketing

Experience Required: Extensive experience in the craft medium you want to sell

Materials Required: Depends upon the craft

Marketing Method: Personal selling

Expected Wages: $4 per hour

Handicrafts can be a wonderful business. Handicrafts can be a terrible business. The good part about making handicrafts is the personal satisfaction you get from selling your own creations. The bad news is that most handicrafts are priced so that the creator gets far less than minimum wage for his or her efforts. If you want to get into handicrafts as a *business,* you need to be very good and also *speedy!* If you sell beautiful handknit sweaters for $20 that cost $15 in yarn and take ten hours to make, you will have earned fifty cents an hour! That's not a business, that's a hobby. Consider handicrafts only if you have a few simple craft items that are easy to make and have a reasonable possibility for volume sales.

For example, let's say you want to make T-shirts for babies, with clever slogans cross-stitched on the chest. If the shirt and embroidery thread cost $2, and it takes you one hour to make a shirt, you'll need to charge at least $6 to cover your labor in order to earn $4 per hour. Six dollars won't even cover the extra time it will take you to SELL the item, so $6 is the bare minimum to charge. What happens if a boutique owner wants to buy your T-shirts in quantities, but feels they're worth only $4 each? If you can't negotiate the owner up to at least $6, DON'T DO IT! Chances are small that you could finish a shirt in less than one hour, even with a quantity order. You would wind up earning less than $2 an hour. If that's the case, keep cross-stitching as a hobby for friends and family; consider another business idea to make money.

The greatest opportunity in handicrafts exists in personalized items. Everyone wants to buy special things made just for them, with their name on it. The key to selling is to hit upon a unique craft idea. Prepare a few samples, then approach boutique owners. See if they will display your samples and take orders, splitting the profits between you and their store. If so, they'll call you to place customer orders. This method makes a lot more sense than making up your craft item with every conceivable name hoping they all sell. The personalized market is especially hot for baby gifts. Almost every parent buys at least one item with their son or daughter's name on it.

Another method for selling handicrafts is to work craft fairs. Contact local communities for information on dates and locations. Go well-stocked with plenty of merchandise. Be sure to take a supply of business cards or leaflets with order information to get additional sales.

Some communities have permanent "flea markets," where you rent a small booth for a reasonable amount of money on weekends. You then must charge enough to cover materials, labor for making the items, labor for your time selling at the booth, *plus* rent.

In the example below, you'll need to charge *at least* $8.60 per shirt to cover all your costs and earn a minimum of $4 per hour. If sales volume falls below the 20 shirt estimate, you'll have to raise your price to cover the costs of running the booth.

Example
Selling Baby T-shirts

Estimated sales per Saturday: 20 shirts

Cost to produce 20 shirts:

Labor, one hour each for 20 shirts @ $4	$80
Materials @ $2 each for 20 shirts	40
Booth rental for one day	20
Labor, eight hours in the booth @ $4	32
Total costs	**$172**

Total Costs Divided By 20 Shirts = $172/20 = $8.60 Per Shirt

There are thousands of ideas to use for a handicrafts business. It's better to stick to one or two things you can make well than to prepare a huge line of products. Some ideas are listed below:

1. Embroidery/cross-stitch Baby items: T-shirts, bibs, sleepers, diaper covers, wall hangings, quilts, gowns, caps, birth announcement wall hanging. Other: personalized shirts, camera straps, guitar straps, wall hanging containing marriage or anniversary information.

2. Fabric painting Any of the baby items listed above, plus any item of clothing for children or adults, table place mats, napkins, aprons, towels, Christmas stockings, sneakers.

3. Knitting Forget it! Unless you own a knitting machine, almost any item you can think of to make would take more labor hours than someone would be willing to pay for.

4. Calligraphy Paint names to personalize already-made products such as purses, duffel bags, lunch buckets, toothbrushes, children's furniture, desk accessories, dishes, hair accessories, you name it! The paint you use will depend upon the item you are painting. Check with a local craft or hobby store to find the right paint suitable for metal, fabric, plastic or wood. You don't want your calligraphy wearing off or coming out in the wash.

5. Needlepoint Personalized glasses cases, chair covers, camera straps, book marks.

6. Woodworking Children's furniture, hat/coat racks, cookbook racks, children's toys, picture frames.

7. Ceramics Usually not a profitable business unless you buy already-fired pieces and simply paint or letter names on them. Baby booties with birth information, plate and cup sets personalized for toddlers, or wedding bells with names and dates are popular items.

8. Jewelry making

9. Sewing Any unique, colorful or artistic item of clothing. Good opportunities exist for costume-making or holiday items. Also consider applique work on sweat shirts or baby clothes, or using your machine for monogramming initials.

This is an extremely short list of available opportunities. Scout craft magazines and craft fairs for additional ideas.

Idea
34

Tutoring

Job Description: Education expert

Personal Traits Required: Patience and ability to communicate well with children

Experience Required: Straight A's in the field you will tutor

Materials Required: Books, workbooks

Marketing Method: Door-to-door flyer, posters at school

Expected Wages: $4 to $10 per hour

Tutoring children is a science and an art. You need to have a distinguished record in the subject you plan to tutor – only straight A's in that field will do. That's just the beginning of what's required. Perhaps more important than expertise in a subject is ability to communicate with and motivate clients. You will be asked to succeed where professional teachers have failed—helping students get good grades.

It's much easier to find tutoring jobs if you have an impressive list of credentials. You must have at least three basic skills to get started:

▶ Straight A's in the subject you will tutor

▶ At least a B+/A− grade point average in your other subjects

▶ Experience teaching or counseling children—summer camp counselor, Sunday school teacher, bible school teacher, educational practicum classes in school

▶ At least three excellent academic references

In addition to the basics listed above, it would also help if you have academic awards such as membership in the honor society or dean's list; a high score if you've already taken your SAT or ACT test; or any other scholastic or citizenship achievement award. Prior tutoring experience, even for smaller sisters or brothers, would be a definite plus.

Assemble a reference file of letters to carry with you to show to prospective clients. If you don't have any previous tutoring experience, take letters describing your outstanding academic ability written by your principal, counselor or teachers. The letter should include the full name, address and telephone number of your references so prospective clients can contact them. If you have tutored before, ask previous clients for a recommendation letter for your file. These testimonials will help sell your service more than anything else.

How can you get the experience to be a good tutor? Before you begin tutoring as a business, practice working with a small child for at least a few weeks. If you do a good job, you might acquire just the reference letter you need to get started. You may find some surprises, too. Some people are excellent scholars but discover they can't work with kids or even hate it. That's critically important to know *before* you begin tutoring as a business. Also, you need to understand the learning process and some child psychology. Many high schools offer education courses. A community library should have a large section on education, with books specializing in each subject area. You'll even find excellent books on tutoring.

Once you've decided you do indeed have the skills and experience necessary to be a good tutor, then it's time to make some decisions about a tutoring business. Where will you provide the tutoring sessions? Many parents will want you to teach at the child's home, so they can keep an eye on their youngster (and you). This is not necessarily the best environment in which to tutor. Face it, for the most part, the kids you will be tutoring have learning problems and low grades—and maybe problems at home, too. Some kinds think tutoring is a form of punishment, especially if the parent is looming at close range. If you have a quiet corner in your house that you can use regularly, then that's probably the best place for a tutoring session. You could also meet in a quiet corner of a library. Get the kids OUT of their environment to stimulate learning.

What about the length of the tutoring sessions? The ideal session is one hour, once or twice a week. Stick to that unless the child is very small, is hyperactive or has difficulty concentrating.

Before starting the serious business of tutoring, spend some time getting to know the child. Ask him or her to bring homework samples to your first session. Quiz your student about the problems he is having, and why. Go through current textbooks and workbooks to get a feel of where the student is and should be in terms of academic progress. Spend time between the first session and the next analyzing the student's strengths and weaknesses, and prepare your lesson plans accordingly.

Beyond the initial work of analyzing your students' academic strengths and weaknesses, make them feel warm, welcome and comfortable with you. Your students may view you very negatively at first. After all, they are exposing their greatest weakness to you, their failure to achieve academically. That may make them very uncomfortable, embarrassed, even hostile. To overcome this, find out what they really like to do, and what they do best. Concentrate on their strengths and successes rather than dwell on their failures.

The professional tutor always has a lesson plan prepared prior to the session. This not only helps the child, but even the simplest of lesson plans will make the session go much easier for you. If you want the child to enjoy the work, don't just review the textbook he's already using (and probably hates). Develop some fun learning games. Try new and fresh learning materials. Education books in the library usually contain great ideas geared to specific age groups.

Professional tutors charge anywhere from $15 to $40 per hour. If you have no experience, start on the low end of wages, say $4 or $5 per hour. Once you get a few glowing recommendations, you'll be able to raise your rates.

The best way to advertise is in your neighborhood, with door-to-door flyers. Your ad should mention any honors or other credentials you have, including your experience. It should also list your prices, which should help you sell your services. Pick one particular subject and one narrow age group, such as math for 4th, 5th and 6th grades. Besides the door-to-door flyer, check at schools close to you for the age group you want to tutor. Leave your name and information with teachers there. They may recommend you to parents. Another method of getting your name out would be to put up posters at day care centers that handle your age group.

Idea
35

Making Music

Job Description: Professional musician

Personal Traits Required: Outgoing personality for performing and marketing

Experience Required: EXPERT level of musical ability

Materials Required: Your instrument, sheet music

Marketing Method: Personal selling, using an agent

Expected Wages: $5 to $10 per hour

When people think of teenage musicians, they usually picture rock and roll bands. In actuality, rock and roll bands are one of the WORST ways to make money. Ninety-nine percent of teen rock groups don't earn enough to pay for their expensive equipment, simply because there are not enough performance opportunities. Rock and roll bands ARE fun, but usually not a practical business venture.

Your money-making opportunities lie elsewhere, in solo or small ensemble work. Attempt to set up a business with your musical talents only if you are *really good*—all-state champion material. If you want to be a professional musician, you'll spend more of your time marketing than actually performing, so you'll also need self-confidence and poise. No matter how good you are, you won't be a business success unless you can walk into someone's office, look them straight in the eye, and convince them you're the next Barbra Streisand or Huey Lewis. Remember, you'll probably be selling and performing to an older crowd. Dressing and acting like a spaced-out heavy metal freak isn't a good marketing tactic. Keep outlandish makeup and clothing to the stage, and only if it's appropriate to your music and your performance venue.

One of the best opportunities for finding regular work is through religious organizations. If you can play the piano, organ, or sing solos, contact local churches and synagogues for work. Try sending letters to all the organizations in the community, offering your musical talents for services or weddings, either as a regular performer or as a substitute. Don't try the large cathedrals with 4,000 members. They'll have plenty of musicians with heavy-duty music degrees. Aim for the smaller organizations. A church organist in a small church usually gets paid $30 to $60 per Sunday, regardless of the age of the performer. If you can play hymns on sight and have a large repertoire, you can qualify for the job.

Weddings are a good market to tap for any serious musician, whether doing solo or ensemble work. For example, if you play the trumpet, consider forming a brass quartet or quintet. You need only six to ten standard pieces to play for weddings. Advertise your services directly to churches, chapels and synagogues. Also, post advertisements where people buy or rent wedding clothes. It's a good idea to have a tape recording ready to play for prospective clients.

If you work with a group, you'll need to coordinate exactly who does what. Draw up some rules and make sure everyone agrees to them. One of the biggest problems with a music group is division of responsibility. *Every* member of the group must take responsibility for a portion of the group's duties, and must make every effort to show up for engagements on time.

If you play the piano, harp, classical guitar, electronic organ, or sing, consider performing in local restaurants. Market your services by sending out letters, or making personal visits. When making sales calls, have a tape recording ready or be fully prepared to perform. A restaurant owner will be skeptical of your abilities at your age. To make a good impression, visit during off-peak hours when the manager won't be too busy to talk, such as 10:30 in the morning or mid-afternoon. Better yet, call ahead for an appointment.

Another marketing technique is to contact local hotels and motels large enough to have meeting and banquet rooms. If you have an ensemble such as a string quartet or small dance band, offer your services for weddings, banquets and parties. The hotel manager usually won't be able to say "yes" or "no" right on the spot, so leave a leaflet or business card with your prices and a phone number.

If you live in a large city, you may try finding an agent to represent you. Agents are responsible for finding work for you, and normally charge ten to fifteen percent of your earnings. Check in your local telephone directory, usually under theatrical agencies, or ask professional musicians if they have an agent to recommend. Caution: Usually, you can't get an agent unless you're very good and are already performing successfully.

Idea

36

Bicycle Repair

Job Description: Bike mechanic

Personal Traits Required: Mechanical aptitude

Experience Required: A proven ability to repair most bike problems

Materials Required: Basic tools, lubricants, tire pump, tire patches

Marketing Method: Door-to-door flyers, posters

Expected Wages: $5 per hour and up

In the good old days, people bought bicycles at bike shops. Now, the majority of bikes are bought at large discount chains or toy stores. Most of these stores don't have service or repair facilities. It's very difficult to find a good bike mechanic, so there's probably an opportunity to set up shop in your community.

To be a bike repair specialist, you need above-average mechanical ability plus familiarity with most makes and models of bicycles. Practice on all your neighbors' bikes before you go into business. Most bike repairs, short of repairing severe frame damage from a crash, should be within your capabilities. However, it takes practice, patience and mechanical skill to perform repairs quickly and efficiently enough to earn a good living.

To be in the bike maintenance and repair business, you'll need a few basic pieces of equipment. You can't possibly stock all the gears, tires and parts for every make of bike. If a customer needs a part, order it. Don't spend money to stock a huge inventory. After all, even the largest bike repair shops can't afford to keep all the pieces for *every* make of bike in inventory at all times. So what DO you need? Experience will tell you what you need to work with, but here are the basic tools of the trade:

▶ Spray lubricant, such as WD-40 or LPD

▶ Medium weight oil, such as SAE 30

▶ Bicycle grease

▶ Kerosene for soaking bike chains and for general cleaning

▶ Tire pump

▶ Tire patch kit

▶ Tire pressure gauge

▶ Set of metric socket wrenches

▶ Screwdrivers—flathead and Phillips varieties

▶ Chain rivet remover for removing bike chains

▶ Cone wrench for removing wheel hubs

▶ Spoke wrench kit for tightening or loosening spokes

These are just the basics. Scout out the tools at a large bike dealership, and practice with them to see what works best.

There's not space available here to describe all the repairs necessary for bikes. Any library or bookstore should have a good, general bicycle repair manual. Study it thoroughly, and practice on your own bike. Join a bike club if there's one in your town. Fellow members may be able to provide advice or assistance on particularly difficult repairs. Also, if you have a local full-service bike shop, feel free to pick the brains of the repair technicians there. You'll probably be ordering parts from them. Free advice on installation and maintenance problems is usually provided cheerfully along with your parts order.

The best way to sell your service is to provide "package deals." People neglect or ignore bicycle maintenance, either because they don't know how to do it themselves or can't find anyone to do it for them. In the spring, offer a special "Spring Service Check" for a package price. Some of the features to include are:

▶ Thorough cleaning

▶ Check tires

▶ Check spoke tension

▶ Check that wheel rims are true

▶ Make sure all nuts are securely tightened

▶ Oil and lubricate all moving parts

▶ Remove the chain, clean in kerosene, remount and lubricate

▶ Check grease on crank bearings

▶ Check brake shoes, clean thoroughly

▶ Check condition of cables

▶ Check kickstand mounting

▶ Remove, clean, remount and grease pedals

▶ Remove rust and wax paint surfaces

Note: It's best to clean the bike before you begin repairs! You may find that, in performing a spring checkup, your customer's bike needs parts. It's up to you to decide if you'll get into the parts business. Prepare a list of parts that need replacing. Then, either hand the customer the parts list so that he can go elsewhere for repair, or draw up a quotation—the price you would charge for parts and repair. *Don't* ever go ahead and replace parts without permission from your customers. They should have a reliable estimate of cost before you go ahead and replace parts.

If business picks up, consider contacting a wholesale parts supplier to cut your costs. Call bike manufacturers directly for information. Try the national toll-free directory assistance at 1-800-555-1212 and check to see if a manufacturer has a free long distance telephone number. Whether you order parts from a local bike shop, the manufacturer, or a wholesale supplier, make sure you know the time it takes to get parts.

Run through the above list of maintenance items a few times on your own bike, or a friend's, to time yourself. Professional bike shops charge anywhere from $12 to $30 an hour for bike maintenance and repair. With practice, you should be able to do everything on this list in three to four hours. If you charged a flat fee, say $15 to $30, you should be able to earn in the $5 to $10 range per hour. Another good time to advertise this package special would be in the fall, just before customers put their bikes away for winter storage.

One advantage you have with a neighborhood service is that you're close to your customers. You can offer free pickup and delivery service, something no bike shop can match. By picking up the bike and riding it from and to your customer's house, you'll be able to assess its problems better and give it a test drive before you return it. (If you're picking up a bike that needs repair, take along a tire pump and repair kit just in case.)

The door-to-door flyer is probably the best method of advertising for a neighborhood business. If you want to expand, use posters or place clasified ads in the newspapers. Offer your services at stores that carry bikes but don't have repair shops, such as any K-Mart, Target or toy store. Ask if you can post an ad or business card in the bicycle department, and ask the salespeople if they will refer clients to you.

Another opportunity these days is basic new bike assembly. Because most bikes are now sold in large stores without service departments, rather than in bike shops, the vast majority of bikes come in boxes, unassembled. Many parents are daunted by do-it-yourself bike assembly. Pay a visit to the bike departments of large stores that don't have service shops. Let them know you are available for bike assembly (and repair). Ask if they will refer clients to you, or if you can leave a business card or poster in a prominent spot. They might even consider allowing you to put bikes together in the back storeroom, especially during peak sales times such as early spring or Christmas.

Idea

37

Telemarketing

Job Description: Telephone salesperson

Personal Traits Required: You must have an excellent speaking voice, easily understood over the telephone. Also, you'll need some basic writing skills to compose a sales pitch to deliver over the phone

Experience Required: None

Materials Required: Access to a telephone, pad and pencil

Marketing Method: Direct marketing to small businesses

Expected Wages: $5 to $10 per hour

Selling goods and services to the public via the telephone is the wave of the future. Door-to-door selling has practically disappeared in the United States for two basic reasons:

1.   Most women now work outside the home.

2.   Many people are reluctant to open the door to a stranger.

Because of this trend, you have the opportunity to help out small businesses in your area.

Telemarketing is simply calling people on the telephone to sell them something. This is a GREAT business because you can work right out of your house and make the calls whenever it is convenient for you. Most small businesses can't afford to hire a person dedicated to telemarketing. *You* can increase any company's profits by making sales calls on the phone.

Depending upon the type of product or service, sometimes you can do telemarketing *at no cost to the company*. You can either charge by the hour, by the number of people contacted or by charging a "commission." Let's say you are working for a carpet cleaning company. You call 100 people. It takes you three hours to do this. You could charge a fee per hour, let's say $6, for a total of $18. Or, you could charge 20¢ per call, for a total of $20.

The best way might be to charge only for "success." For example, out of 100 people, you find 4 who want to set up an appointment for cleaning. Then, you could charge $5 for each appointment made, or $20. This last method, charging a fee for each successful contact made, is probably the best way to set your price. That way, the business owner only pays when you increase his or her profits, so it doesn't require any risk. He or she doesn't pay to have you sit on the phone, and they won't worry that you are just wasting time.

The best way to market this service is to visit the small business owner in person. Set up an appointment by telephone first. Before you arrive, write down a short, one-minute sample telephone sales pitch geared specifically to that business. Go over it with the business owner. See if he has any special offers or sales he might want to feature in the sales pitch.

If YOU will be scheduling appointments, you'll need access to their appointment book. If the owner wants to do the scheduling himself, tell the phone client that he will be contacted shortly to set up the appointment. Then hand the list of names and numbers to the owner to follow up.

Here's a list of local businesses that could increase their sales or fundraising by telemarketing:

- Air conditioning/heating maintenance or repair
- Banks
- Beauty salons
- Carpet cleaners
- Caterers
- Charity organizations—for fundraising
- Churches—for fundraising or to advertise a special event

▶ Day care centers

▶ Dentists

▶ Diet centers

▶ Dry cleaners

▶ Fireplace/chimney cleaners

▶ Gutter repair/replacement—especially to clean out leaves in the fall

▶ Health studios

▶ Home repair/remodelers

▶ House cleaning

▶ Insurance agents

▶ Lawn/landscaping services

▶ Painters

▶ Pest control

▶ Photography studios

▶ Real estate companies

▶ Restaurants

▶ Roofing contractors

▶ Schools—for fundraising

▶ Security companies

▶ Stock brokers

▶ Tax accountants—especially from January through April

▶ Travel agents

▶ Window washers

You don't necessarily have to be selling a specfic product or service. You might simply invite customers to a special event, such as a store opening or a church fundraiser. In that case, charge by the number of people contacted. Usually, you can use your community telephone book.

Sometimes, you may not want to contact the whole town but only a special group of people most likely to buy. For example, if you are making sales calls for an office supply company, you'll probably just want to contact businesses in the area. Use the Yellow Pages to find telephone numbers, or check with the local Chamber of Commerce to see if they have a specialized listing.

After preparing the sales pitch with your customer, go over it with them to make sure they approve of the message. It's always more effective for telemarketing if you have something special to offer, such as a half-price sale. Practice the message several times before you begin making sales calls. Phone up friends or neighbors to see if they can understand you. Speak slowly but with enthusiasm no matter how many times you make the same call.

Be prepared to answer questions, but if you get stumped, refer them directly to the business owner and give them a telephone number. You'll want to sound as adult as you can, so try to speak in low, business-like tones. Vary the pitch of your delivery so you don't sound like a robot and put people to sleep.

The best time to make telephone calls is when people arrive home from work, usually between six and eight P.M. Don't call after nine o'clock—you don't want to interrupt bedtime. Unless you are making calls to businesses, you won't have much success calling during the day.

When making calls, keep track of how many people you've contacted. Record the names and telephone numbers of "successful" contacts. Write up a report with this information for the business owner so he or she can check your progress on a regular basis.

Idea

38

Calligraphy

Job Description: Pen-and-ink artist

Personal Traits Required: Neatness and precision

Experience Required: A course in calligraphy plus extensive practice

Materials Required: Special calligraphy pens and paper

Marketing Method: Posters, direct selling, classified ads

Expected Wages: $5 to $10 per hour

If you are a skilled calligrapher, consider turning it into a business. Calligraphy is the art of handwriting in an artistic, elegant way. Many public schools offer basic calligraphy training. Also check local community or vocational schools for instruction courses. If you have an artistic bent, you may be able to pick up the skills you need by studying books on the subject and practicing.

The calligrapher is in demand for addressing formal invitations and announcements for weddings, graduations, bar or bas mitzvahs, births, new addresses and for parties. Many fine restaurants use menus prepared by a calligrapher rather than a printer. Posters or other advertising are sometimes done with calligraphy.

The trick to this business is finding clients. The best place to go is local printers. They are the ones who produce all the invitations that need addressing. Take some samples of your work and a price list to all the printers in your area. If they allow it, prepare a beautiful poster with samples of your calligaphy and hang it in a prominent spot near the printer's front door.

Another marketing method is to visit businesses that might need your services. For example, find a menu from a local restaurant and prepare a sample, using your calligraphy. See if you can sell the restaurant owner by showing how beautiful a customized, hand-lettered menu can be.

Offer your services to local advertising agencies. They may need your work for brochures or print ads. Some calligraphers advertise in the Yellow Pages or in the classified ad section of the newspaper under "Personal Services."

Another way to market your calligraphy is to prepare lovely, framed poems or famous sayings and sell them at craft fairs, gift shops and boutiques. Another popular use of framed calligraphy is hand-lettering biblical or other religious verses or poems, which can be sold in religious gift or book stores. Hand-letter the words on antique parchment or heavy card stock; then slip the finished piece into a pre-made frame.

Make sure the words you use aren't under copyright. All literature is protected for the sole use and profit of the author and publisher during the author's lifetime plus fifty years after the author dies. After that, anyone is free to use the material in any way they wish. Any poem, essay or piece of literature you want to use should have a copyright date in the front of the book.

You could also sell custom-made, framed birth or wedding announcements. Put up samples at baby or wedding boutiques. There are a number of other baby items you could personalize with calligraphy, such as ceramic baby booties, baby dishes, rockers, step stools, clothing, Christmas ornaments and bibs. Prepare samples to place in boutiques. The boutique owner will take orders for you. In return, you'll split the profits with the owner.

If you want to be successful, you'll need to master several calligraphy styles, such as Old English, and produce them consistently. Once you are well-practiced, establish prices by timing yourself. For example, if it takes you five minutes to prepare one addressed envelope, you could price your service at 60¢ per envelope and earn $7.20 per hour. Before setting your price, check around to see if you have any established competition, and try to undercut their prices.

Ventures with Your Personal Computer

39. Word Processing

40. Mailing Labels/ Customer Data Base

41. Personalized Greeting Cards

42. Computer Consultant

Unless you already have a computer and basic computer skills, *skip this section.* The only exception is if you and your family are already considering buying a computer for family use. The business ideas in this section can help you pay for a family machine. However, this book does *not* recommend buying a complete computer setup just to start up a part-time, home-based business. You can't reasonably expect to cover the costs of a full computer setup, much less turn a profit, unless you plan to keep at the business longer than two years.

If you are determined to buy a computer for use in a small business, consider buying a good, used machine. You can find perfectly adequate used equipment for less than $1,000, sometimes for a few hundred dollars, printer and all! A new IBM or Apple system would cost you in the $3,000 to $6,000 range.

What size personal computer do you need to set up one of the business ideas in this section? Just some general advice here: a TI/99A is too small. Any machine that only uses tape cartridges or cassettes for storage will probably be too small. That leaves out almost all computer systems costing less than $500. Their use is primarily for games and home learning. The minimum requirements for a computer for use in one of the business ideas in this section would be:

▶ At least 128K in RAM (random access memory). If you'll be running any large-scale data bases in Idea #40, you'll need more. A simple mailing label business won't need anything more than 128K, but the sophisticated data base programs need 512K to run properly.

▶ Two disk drives, or one disk drive and at least a 1M hard disk.

▶ A printer. Each business idea contains printer requirements.

None of the applications in this section requires the latest, biggest, most sophisticated machine. Even an old Apple II+ would do.

Do you have to be a programming wizard? No—and yes. You need to know your way around a computer keyboard, and have some basic typing ability. Some practice working with computer equipment is important. Idea #39, Word Processing, primarily requires good typing skills. It takes about three weeks of solid practice to familiarize yourself with a word processing software package such as Microsoft Word or Wordstar. No "programming" is really involved. You just need to learn some basic computer commands. Idea #41, Personalized Greeting Cards, is done with an inexpensive software package such as Printshop. Anyone can sit down and produce greeting cards in minutes using this program. The program is self-explanatory; you don't even need to use the manual to design and print your own cards. Ideas #40 and #42 do take a little more computer expertise. The data base software used in #40 is relatively complex and you must practice before you understand its full capabilities. Computer Consultant, Idea #42, takes expert knowledge of software packages and experience.

This section contains only a few ideas for making money with your computer. The home-based computer industry is booming. Your library or bookstore should have several books with money-making ideas.

If you are going to run a business based on your home computer, make sure you have reliable equipment, much more reliable than you'd need for just personal use. Find a good service dealer in your area that stocks parts, so that if you DO have a breakdown, you'll be back up and running in a matter of hours or a few days, instead of weeks. This is easier said than done. Most computer stores are in the business of selling only. It's very difficult to find good computer repair technicians. If you're mechanically inclined, read up on simple computer trouble shooting, so that you can fix minor problems yourself. Consider signing up for a long-term maintenance contract with your dealer. It's like an insurance policy. For a fixed fee at the beginning of the year, your service dealer will fix all problems, including all labor and parts. Some agreements even include service calls to your house. These agreements are expensive, but so is computer repair. Most repair bills start at $50 and go up from there. Some computers rarely, if ever, break down; it's difficult to know in advance if you're going to have problems. One thing you can do to cut down on maintenance is to perform regular "preventive" maintenance. Your computer and printer manuals will contain preventive maintenance procedures you can do yourself. Follow them carefully. Take extra steps to keep your equipment clean. Dust your printer regularly, following the manual instructions. Buy a disk drive cleaning kit and use it. Simply keeping your equipment clean will prevent many problems.

Have an alternative plan available in case of computer breakdown. The best, and usually cheapest, form of insurance is to know where you can locate a spare machine in case yours breaks down. Community libraries and local colleges sometimes rent computer time for a reasonable hourly fee. Check around with local dealers to see if they rent machines like yours on a short-term basis. Usually you can get your machine repaired quickly, but if a part is out of stock, you might have to wait several weeks for a replacement. This would ruin your business unless you had a spare machine available.

Another important aspect of the computer business is to *take care of your customer's data.* Make backup copies of *everything!* Keep copies of original input material from your customer so if disaster happens, you can reconstruct the information.

One of the advantages of a computer-based business is that you can take it with you anywhere—to another town if you move, or to college. Plus, the skills you learn are invaluable. Computer experience on your resume will give you a job-hunting edge. You can also turn a computer business into a full-time career.

Idea

39

Word Processing

Job Description: Professional word processor

Personal Traits Required: Top-notch spelling, grammar and English ability. Also, good people skills for dealing with clients.

Experience Required: Advanced typing skills—you should be able to type at least fifty words per minute with very few mistakes.

Materials Required: A computer with plenty of storage, either two floppy disk drives or one drive and a hard disk, paper, good quality printer, ribbons, word processing software

Marketing Method: Classified ads, personal selling

Expected Wages: At least $5 per hour

Go back and review #27, Typing Service, before you read this section. Most of the basic principles of a typing service apply to this business idea as well.

In order to be a professional word processor, you'll need a good word processing (WP) software package. The two most popular are Wordstar, a MicroPro product, and Microsoft Word. These two packages cost several hundred dollars, but they literally do everything. Plus, they have been time-tested by thousands of users and all the "bugs" have been worked out of the programs. Your computer may have come with its own WP package. Several cheaper packages are available. Look in recent issues of computer magazines for ratings of WP products. Since WP is the most popular personal computing application, good articles comparing software packages appear every month.

How do you know if a WP package is adequate for professional use? Some are good only for short memos or letters, so watch out. Here are some feature to look for:

1. Page limits Some software can handle only short reports. You need to have unlimited capability for longer papers.

2. Cut and paste feature This is a standard feature that separates WP from typing on a typewriter. Cut and paste allows you to insert, move or delete words, paragraphs or entire files within a document. Check to make sure your software package has it, and how it works.

3. Form letter, sometimes called "mail merge" capability Many WP packages allow you to create form letters or repetitive documents. This feature lets you print an unlimited number of copies of the same basic document, but allows you to "customize" each one, entering individual information from either the keyboard or a separate file. For example, you could send a newsletter to fifty of your relatives. Using the mail merge capability, you could ask the computer to print fifty copies, inserting a different name at the top of each letter. You could also print business sales letters, changing the address and salutation for each addressee.

4. Global search and replace This WP feature allows you to find and change words or phrases everywhere they appear in a document. For example, you could ask the program to find all references to "Susie Shwartz" you have in a file, and change every one to "Susan Schwartz."

5. Other features Here's a list of features that the expensive WP packages have, that you might need:

- ▶ Automatic margin justification
- ▶ Underlining
- ▶ Boldface
- ▶ Italics
- ▶ Custom headings
- ▶ Variable page numbering options
- ▶ Footnotes

- ▶ Subscripts and superscripts
- ▶ File hierarchy for easy file retrieval
- ▶ Variable tabs or margins
- ▶ Variable print type faces and sizes
- ▶ Spelling checker
- ▶ Thesaurus

The spelling checker can come in quite handy. It will go through a file, count how many words the file contains (really handy if you charge by the word) and print out a list of words that are either misspelled or that the program can't identify. A good spelling checker will have a dictionary of 80,000 words on file, to which you can add several thousand of your own. Spelling checkers can't possibly include names of people, cities, slang, or technical words, so when your list of errors comes out, it will look something like this:

antediluvian; Aunt Sally; Dimebox, Texas; neoarsphenamine; blankeet, parachoot

Only the last two are real errors. You can choose to change any or all of the words, or leave them alone.

Only a daisy wheel printer, ink jet printer or laser printer will produce results as good as a typewriter. Daisy wheel printers are *extremely* slow, as slow as ten characters per second. Ink jet printers and laser printers produce great results, but they are expensive and break down a lot. Most home computer printers are the dot matrix variety. These are really fast, and have proven to be more reliable than other printer types. Dot matrix is probably adequate for typing school papers or mailing labels, but if you want to expand into the business world, you'll need a higher quality, more expensive printer. The new technology dot matrix printer with a twenty-four pin printhead (rather than the old nine-pin printhead) has recently been introduced by most major printer companies. These are slightly more expensive than the old nine-pin variety; most are in the $450 to $800 range. However, their results should be adequate for all but your pickiest customers.

Word processing gives you a much wider range of typing opportunities than a plain typewriter. You can specialize in long documents that require numerous revisions, such as college papers. Or, you can tap the business market by specializing in form letters. Sometimes, all you need is one or two big customers who will give you all their business correspondence. Here are some ideas you can try to tap the business/commercial market:

Type of Customer	Type of document
Academic – contact local schools	Reports, theses
Restaurants and coffee shops	Menus
Writers and writer's groups	Books, manuscripts
Real estate agents	Newsletters, property listings
Churches	Newsletters, bulletins
Social clubs	Newsletters
Doctors	Insurance claims, medical reports
Lawyers	Routine contracts

Besides these specific categories, any small business might need additional secretarial support, so check around.

If you plan on marketing to one of the specialized categories listed above, have some samples ready to show prospective clients. You can choose to market your skills by making direct sales calls, or by sending a well-typed and formatted letter advertising your service. It must be absolutely perfect if you are advertising word processing! A classified ad in the local newspaper might draw some customers. Also, posters at local schools and colleges should drum up some business. Remember, if you're going to try to tap the business and professional market, you must look and act the part. When making a sales call, dress like a professional office worker and concentrate on using your best English grammar.

Idea

40

Mailing Labels/ Customer Data Base

Job Description: Computer consultant
Personal Traits Required: You must be extremely careful with customer records and detailed

work. Also, you must have self-confidence and an outgoing personality to market your service.

Experience Required: Personal computing and light typing

Materials Required: Personal computer, good printer, mailing labels, envelopes

Marketing Method: Direct mail, door-to-door or telephone sales

Expected Wages: $5 per hour

Virtually every business, club or religious organization sends out large batches of letters, brochures or other documents to customers or members. Even private individuals sometimes generate large mailings when they send out resumes, newsletters or holiday cards. Keeping track of and updating a long list of addresses for regular mailings can be a time-consuming chore. It's even more of a chore to type or photocopy the same document over and over. Many companies still handle mass mailings this old-fashioned way, preparing each document by hand or with a typewriter. However, if you have a reliable computer with reasonable storage capability (two disk drives or a disk drive and a hard disk), you can provide a modern, streamlined, and most important, *cheaper* method of preparing mass mailings.

If your personal computer has a data base application, you can use it to store general information about clients or to generate mailing lists. A computer makes it easy to keep track of a constantly changing customer list, and print updated mailing labels at a moment's notice.

A data base can do much more than simply generate updated mailing labels. It can also keep track of any number of vital pieces of information critical to your clients, provided your client gives you the basic raw data. For example, for a pediatrician, you could keep a data base that includes patients' birthdays, illnesses, vaccinations, etc. A data base of this type can be easily sorted to find out which children were born in any given month. Such information can be used to print mailing labels and letters to remind parents to schedule their children's annual physical. A search could also be performed to find out which children of which particular age need a certain vaccination. Again, form letters and mailing labels could then be generated to remind parents about the need to vaccinate their youngsters. The capabilities of a data base are limited only by the type of information you include. Sorting, retrieving and printing do *not* require any "programming" per se, just a few simple commands.

Your clients will be the small businesses and organizations in your community that need to save time and secretarial wages when sending regular mailings to changing lists of clients. Most medium and large businesses are already automated. Therefore, you need to aim for non-computerized offices, such as realtors, churches, insurance agents, social clubs, lawyers, doctors, car dealers—any organization that regularly sends mail to its customers, but has no computer.

You need access to a computer with the capacity to store sizeable files on permanent storage. It is recommended that you keep each customer separate, one client per storage diskette. There are many software programs available to generate mailing labels. However, it is extremely easy to program your own in BASIC or PASCAL. You can buy software packages that update and print mailing lists for $20 to $50. However, if you need to keep track of more than just name, address and telephone number, you might need more expensive data base software such as dBASE III by Ashton-Tate. The most expensive data base packages can cost more than $500, but inexpensive packages start around $80. Shop around and compare features for what you really need. A good place to research available packages and their features is in recent issues of personal computing magazines. Your software dealer should allow you to try out a package before you buy.

Your costs are few for this service. Besides the computer equipment and software, you will need:

1. **Gummed mailing labels**—buy in bulk to save money. The current price of a box of 5,000 is around $32.

2. **Ribbons.** Computer mail-order services usually have the best prices, and offer quantity discounts.

3. **Floppy (5¼ inch) or the new 3½ inch diskettes.** You'll need two per customer, one with the original data and one for a backup. Prices vary widely depending upon the storage media and the vendor you select. Again, the mail-order computer supplier typically has the best price.

If you also offer form letters generated from a data base, you might need stationery and envelopes, although your customer may prefer to supply you with the company's letterhead stationery.

The best way to determine your pricing is to call around and see what your competition charges. Usually, you won't find much competition; you may have to call to a larger town to find a mailing list or data base service. If you establish your prices at 30 to 50 percent lower than the competition, with your low overhead, you'll probably earn good money. For example, recently a company in a large city charged these prices for a basic mailing label service:

▶ $50 one-time-only fee to set up a mailing list of up to 300 people

▶ $30 a month to store the list, regardless of whether any printing was needed

▶ 15 cents per name addition, change or deletion

▶ 15 cents per mailing label printed

If you keep data bases with more complicated information, you'll need to develop a price list for printing form letters or printing out the data base itself. Once again, the best way to determine prices for a customer data base service is to call the competition.

The key to developing a good computer business is *reliability*. Besides the few tips listed at the beginning of this section, keep out of trouble by:

▶ making a backup of each customer's file

▶ keeping a copy of the original input data

▶ giving your customers a hard copy for their records and to verify your work, and

▶ asking your customers to proofread the list before you print any mailing labels.

Because your target market will be small businesses, your advertising needs to be professional. A well-written, neatly typed business letter generated on your home computer should be sufficient, or you could have a mailer typeset at your local printer. A mailer should cost you between $10 to $50 for typesetting plus a few cents per copy. Add to this the expense of envelopes and stamps. If you are advertising computerized mailing labels, the sample mailing labels you send to prospective clients must be of the highest quality. Try an unusual label in a traffic-stopping color—your computer supply company stocks labels on tractor-feed strips in a rainbow of colors and sizes. You can develop a list of prospects by speaking with your local Chamber of Commerce. They should have information on local businesses organized by type and size of business. Also, check the Yellow Pages. Door-to-door selling to small businesses can be quite effective, particularly if you have some sample work ready to show. Selling your service by telephone is another alternative, although it may be difficult to explain your service adequately over the phone. You will probably need to educate prospective clients by explaining just what you and your computer can do for them:

▶ Stress the importance of updating client records regularly and keeping these records well organized.

▶ Remind clients of the cost of paying office help to keep up such a list and type hundreds of envelopes every time the business wants to contact all its customers by mail.

▶ Present yourself as a computer pro; stress that your client does not need to know a thing about computers. You will do all the work. Your client simply provides the customer information.

▶ Offer a quick turnaround time for producing an updated list or generating labels for envelopes.

Besides providing a mailing list service, you could offer other, related service with your computer. For example, you can update your clients' Rolodex files. (Rolodex files are the small, handy card files kept next to millions of business phones. The files contain names, addresses and phone numbers of business contacts.) The Rolodex company now offers file cards printed on computer tractor feed paper for automated updating and printing. They even offer a good software package for mailing list or Rolodex card updating.

Idea

41

Personalized
Greeting Cards

Job Description: Greeting card designer

Personal Traits Required: A poetic nature and an artistic bent

Experience Required: Rudimentary computer skills

Materials Required: Computer, one disk drive, good quality printer, colorful stationery

Marketing Method: Direct sales, newspaper ads, posters

Expected Wages: At least $5 per hour

One of the most fun and useful computer software packages to come along in recent years is a basic package that designs and prints greeting cards. The first package on the market was Printshop, but now there are several packages. Printshop and others, such as Printmaster, are available in the $30 to $60 range. Besides greeting cards, they can also generate 8½ by 11 inch signs, huge banners, stationery and calendars. These greeting card packages allow you to print countless combinations of print styles with graphics and fancy borders. Some of the many graphics (computer-generated drawings) available are birthday cakes, storks, hearts, musical notes, pumpkins, wedding bells and animals. You can print these pre-designed graphics in a number of sizes right on a greeting card you design yourself. Or, the program will allow you to design your own graphics.

A greeting card you buy in a store these days costs anywhere from 75 cents to five dollars. You could probably charge $3 to $5 for a personalized card you design and print yourself. It shouldn't take you more than ten minutes to set up a card and print it. The software package is so easy to use, anyone can sit down in front of a computer and print nice-looking cards in just a few minutes. All the instructions you need are in front of you on the computer screen at all times.

The only other cost you have, besides the computer hardware and software, is paper. Printshop sells its own line of colorful computer tractor-feed paper and envelopes. Actually, any 8½ by 11 inch stationery will do; it's not necessary to use the more expensive tractor-feed paper.

Your best market might be at school. Prepare a number of samples and be ready to show them around. You could also pass around door-to-door flyers in the neighborhood, prepared using the actual software package. Besides standard greeting cards, here are a few other products you can generate with your software package:

- Personalized valentines
- Baby announcements
- Campaign posters
- Graduation announcements
- Wedding invitations
- Party invitations
- 8½ by 11 inch posters for advertising
- Signs for neighborhood garage sales
- Signs to post in car windows "For sale by owner"
- Menu covers

▶ Party banners for birthdays and special occasions

▶ 8½ by 11 inch flyers for door-to-door advertising

▶ Report covers

▶ Personalized stationery and note cards

If you don't generate enough business at school and in the neighborhood, consider placing ads in your local newspaper.

Idea
42

Computer Consultant

Job Description: Profesional computer educator

Personal Traits Required: Good analytical skills and ability to communicate

Experience Required: Expert knowledge of computers and software package(s)

Materials: A computer system

Marketing Method: Direct selling, newspaper ads

Expected Wages: At least $8 per hour

Don't set yourself up in business as a computer consultant *unless* you know a lot about computer hardware systems and software. However, if you do, you can earn terrific wages and launch a career that can last a lifetime, either on a part-time or full-time basis.

Opportunities for earning money as a consultant on a personal computer don't lie in real "programming," that is, inventing your programs from the ground up. The real money-making opportunities stem from what you know about software packages that students, professionals and small businesses use every day. Some of the popular software packages today are pfs:File, Lotus 1-2-3, dBase, Microsoft Word, Visicalc, Wordstar, and Symphony. Besides software packages, many people have trouble learning the basic IBM operating system called MS-DOS. Countless books and classes on the subject indicate a crying need for operating system training.

If you are an expert in a popular software package, and have good communication skills, consider setting yourself up as a computer consultant. Many people own personal computer (PC) systems that sit and collect dust, or aren't being utilized at their full potential. Typically, the reason is that PC owners don't understand how to use software packages, or how to adapt them to their particular needs. Your opportunity lies with one-on-one sessions with PC owners—to teach them how to use software and the variety of applications appropriate to their needs.

The first step in becoming a computer consultant is to have *thorough* understanding of at least one software package. You must have worked extensively with the package, and understand how to use all its advanced features. Then, study every book and magazine article you can find about the software's applications for personal, professional and business users. Next, you'll need to know any special differences the software package has when run on different computer systems. Normally, the software looks and acts the same on all computer systems—but you'll need to check. You can take most popular software packages for a "test drive" at large computer stores.

Once you've acquired this expert knowledge, you're ready to begin your consulting career. The next step is finding customers. Most computer consultants charge at least $35 per hour for one-on-one sessions with clients. If you charge $8 to $10, you'll be a real bargain! You can choose to conduct sessions in your home or at your client's place. Here are some ideas for locating clients:

1. Students Offer lessons to your schoolmates. The best curriculum for students might be a basic beginning computer training session. If there's a demand, you can specialize in one or two software packages. You can put up posters at other schools in your area to expand your business. Don't forget the local vocational or community colleges. At your own school, word of mouth is usually the best form of advertising.

2. Churches Many churches are now automating their records with PCs. A church is one of the least likely places to have PC-trained employees. Call, stop by, or send a letter to area churches.

3. Small busineses Large companies typically have their own in-house PC training programs. Your opportunity for finding business clients will be with smaller firms, such as realtors, brokers, insurance agents and local merchants. Tapping the local business market usually involves "networking"—developing contacts in the business community. Discuss your business with adults, distribute business cards, ask for recommendations, get the word out!

4. Professionals and self-employed people The professional market can probably be reached only through advertising. Try putting up posters or your business card at large office buildings. Newspaper ads might work, too, but they're expensive. Home-based businesses are becoming more popular, and many professionals use computers at home. You could try door-to-door flyers to reach them.

Ventures with Transportation

43. Courier Delivery Service

44. Janitor Service

45. Chauffeur Service

46. General Errand Service

47. Refreshment Wagon

This section is for teenagers who have reliable transportation for use either as a basis for a business, or as a means to get to their customers. Most of the other ideas in this book don't require a vehicle. Some of the ideas in this section need only basic transportation. Ideas #43 and #46 could certainly squeak by with a used moped costing less than $500. Only Idea #45, Chauffeur Service, requires an elaborate vehicle.

Idea

Courier Delivery Service

Job Description: Document/message carrier

Personal Traits Required: You must be prompt and neatly groomed

Experience Required: Only a driver's license

Materials Required: *Any* motorized vehicle, perhaps a pager

Marketing Method: Direct selling, newspaper ads

Expected Wages: $5 per hour

The courier delivery business is in the middle of an all-out war. UPS, Federal Express, Purolator Courier, even the U.S. Post Office are waging a fierce battle for customers. While the big companies slug it out, there's still lots of room for a teen entrepreneur—someone who can zip around town easily and who doesn't have the overhead of national advertising budgets, huge office expenses, and private fleets of airplanes and trucks. Most medium, even small-sized towns could use an inexpensive delivery service to carry documents and small packages from office to office.

Who needs a document delivery service? Many professions generate huge amounts of paper and contracts that must be ferried around to different offices. Real estate agents must get contracts back and forth between lawyers, banks, title companies and customers within the space of a few hours. Lawyers, doctors, financial brokers, insurance agents, and professional secretaries spend a great deal of time moving contracts, documents and packages around town. Even the smallest business needs an occasional hand to carry packages back and forth from the post office. Believe it or not, there are still adults stranded at home without cars who sometimes need a delivery service, particularly for getting packages to the post office.

A recent survey of medium-sized town courier services came up with the following as average prices for delivery fees within the town:

$7 per item   For delivery in over four hours

$9 per item   For delivery under four hours

$12 per item   For *rush* delivery under 90 minutes

These prices are based upon delivery of small packages (less than twenty pounds) or documents.

The following were recent price quotes for delivery to another town or airport within a twenty-five mile radius:

$24 per item   For delivery in over four hours

$30 per item   For delivery in under four hours

$39 per item   For *rush* delivery under 90 minutes

You can cut these prices in half and still make money IF you line up enough customers to keep you busy. Since you will probably be in school, you'll have to restrict your hours to late afternoon during the school year. This will be somewhat inconvenient to your customers, but your low prices can certainly make up for that.

The key to earning good money is to establish a regular clientele. Direct selling to prospective customers will probably be your most effective marketing technique. Visit businesses that are likely targets for your service. Leave a business card or brochure explaining your service and fees. Which businesses are most likely to need you? The following should give you some ideas:

▶ Real estate offices
▶ Law offices
▶ Brokers, such as Merrill Lynch
▶ Insurance agents
▶ Churches
▶ Any small retail business establishment
▶ Retirement homes—many of the occupants don't drive
▶ Professional stenographic or secretarial service companies
▶ Doctors
▶ Dentists
▶ Banks, savings and loans, credit unions
▶ Title companies
▶ Schools—check with yours first!

If you find one or two big customers, you might have enough business to keep you going. Schedule a regular pickup and delivery at a set time each day. If you can't find regular work, your business will be a little more complicated. You'll have several customers who will call you at random, unpredictable times. They'll need to locate you quickly for pickup service, and you'll probably be out on the road. If you want to provide reliable service, you need to provide a method for your customers to reach you in a hurry. There are four methods you could use:

1. A friend or helper to answer your phone at home You could hire a friend, brother or sister, or a helper to answer your home phone. If you worked ten hours a week, and paid a helper $3 an hour to provide the answering service, your costs would be $30 per week. (Don't expect to find someone who'll provide reliable help for free!) You'll then have to call your home phone at regular intervals to get messages.

2. A pager—sometimes called a beeper These handy little machines fit right in your pocket. When customers call your pager phone number, they'll hear a little "BEEP." Then, they enter their own phone number. You'll also hear the beep right after they hang up. If you have a digital pager, it will display the return phone number right on the machine itself.

As soon as you reach a phone, you can return the call. Paging service charges run from $15 to $30 per month, including the rental of the pager.

3. An answering machine You can buy a good, reliable answering machine for under $100. These machines can be hooked up directly to your home phone. You leave a message for customers who call in. Promise to return their calls within a set interval—say, twenty minutes. If your answering machine has a remote playback feature, you can call from any phone and hear what messages have come in since your last call. If you buy an answering machine, you'll probably need your own phone line at home. Your family won't be too keen on your tying up the family phone for business several hours a day. To install another phone line at home will run you at least $20 per month plus installation fees.

4. Professional answering service Most towns have secretarial companies that provide professional answering services. Rates vary. Sometimes, you're charged a flat fee. Some services charge per call received. The advantage of this service is that a pro answers a private line dedicated to *your* business. "Good afternoon, Mercury Messenger Service, may I help you?" is a lot friendlier than the nonpersonal BEEP of a pager or answering machine. The pros can be trusted to take reliable messages. You can call them at regular intervals, and they'll give you the list of people who have called in. Rates for this service can run anywhere from $20 to $50 per month.

While direct selling is the best way to reach the small business and professional market in your town, you might also need to put ads in the paper or phone book to reach a wider market.

Idea

44

Janitor Service

Job Description: Professional custodian

Personal Traits Required: You must have an ability to follow through until all the dirt's gone, plus no allergies to dust.

Experience Required: Basic experience wielding a mop, broom, dust cloth and vacuum cleaner

Materials Required: Reliable transportation. Cleaning supplies can be provided by your clients. Otherwise: mop, pail, broom, rags, cleaning solvents, toilet brush, glass cleaner, vacuum, garbage bags

Marketing Method: Direct sales

Expected Wages: Up to $10 per hour

Most small businesses find it very difficult to locate someone reliable to clean their offices, because not many people want this kind of work. Small operations can't afford to hire people full-time, so they contact professional janitorial or maid service companies. These companies must charge premium prices to cover their office expenses.

A janitor service can be a perfect job for a teenager, both in terms of wages and schedule. You can charge a high price per hour and still undercut the competition. Plus, cleaning is usually done after 5:00 p.m. As long as you have the office, restaurant or building clean by the next morning, it doesn't matter what time you come and go.

A professional janitorial service usually includes:

▶ Dusting all surfaces—desks, bookcases, etc.

▶ Wiping down and disinfecting countertops and tables (for restaurant clients only)

▶ Mopping non-carpeted floors

▶ Wiping down and disinfecting all interior plumbing fixtures, toilets, sinks, countertops

▶ Cleaning ashtrays

▶ Filling paper receptacles: towel dispensers and toilet paper

▶ Emptying waste baskets

▶ Vacuuming carpeted areas

▶ Cleaning glass surfaces (windows are not included)

To do a good job, you *must* be a very picky person. You must pay close attention to your work, and seek out dirt lurking about in corners.

The prices you charge will depend upon the size and type of facility you'll be cleaning. An 800 square foot office without interior plumbing will be a snap to clean compared to a 2,000 square foot restaurant with bathrooms and a complete kitchen setup. Experience will tell you how long it takes to clean various types of buildings. Always check the competition. Use their prices as a guideline. You can usually get well under your competitors' prices and still earn good wages. Here are some examples of janitorial service prices found recently in a medium-sized town:

Example One

Type of facility: 2500 square foot office with two bathrooms

Cleaning provided: Services mentioned above. Service every evening, five days a week. (NOTE: not all services are provided every night. For example, mopping is done only twice a week.) Estimated time spent by janitor on premises: one and ½ hours to two hours per evening.

Typical fee: $35 per night, five nights a week, or $175 per week

Example Two

Type of facility: 800 square foot office, no interior plumbing

Cleaning provided: Dusting, vacuuming, mopping, emptying wastebaskets, glass cleaning, wiping down surfaces as necessary. Service provided once a week, on Saturdays while office closed. Estimated time spent by janitor on the premises: three hours maximum.

Typical fee: $50

In both examples, the professionals were earning in the neighborhood of $17 per hour. (Some of that fee goes to a central office to cover overhead expense.) If you asked for a flat fee, charging $8 an hour for your time, your price would be well below the competition.

One large facility that needs cleaning nightly, such as in Example One, might be all you'd need to earn a good living. Or, you could specialize in small offices that require weekly cleaning and line up four or five customers. Try marketing your services to small office buildings, restaurants, day care centers, social clubs, and churches. It might be wise to leave larger buildings with more complicated cleaning requirements to the big companies. You might try making sales calls to real estate management companies who are in charge of all aspects of building management. They may have one or several locations that need cleaning. You'll probably find you won't need to do much advertising to line up enough customers to keep you busy.

Idea

Chauffeur Service

Job Description: Chauffeur

Personal Traits Required: Very well-groomed and impeccable manners.

Experience Required: A perfect driving record plus a chauffeur's license

Materials Required: Either a nice, roomy new car or a distinctive older vehicle plus a uniform, tuxedo or costume

Marketing Method: Direct selling, posters, newspaper ads

Expected Wages: $5 to $10 per hour

With the rise of TV programs depicting the super-rich, suddenly the chauffeur is "IN!" Arriving in a chauffered vehicle is becoming the preferred method of getting to fancy occasions such as the prom or the homecoming dance.

You can be a chauffeur if you have a reasonably new, roomy car in nice shape or an unusual or distinctive older vehicle. A cherry condition '57 Chevy, Mustang convertible, even an old Cadillac hearse could put you in great demand. You'll also need a perfect driving record plus a chauffeur's license. Check with your local Department of Motor Vehicles to find out about requirements for a chauffeur's license.

Being a chauffeur requires performing your duties with distinction and flair, paying close attention to your client's needs. The special touches will help sell your services. If you're going to be driving for special occasions, here are some tips:

▶ Seat your clients in the back only – never up front with you.

▶ Open and close clients' doors, both for men and women.

▶ Dress for the occasion. Find a suitable uniform, cap, even white gloves. For formal occasions, a tux would be great! Make sure you are perfectly groomed.

▶ Act the part.

▶ Make sure your car has a good sound system, and keep it stocked with a variety of music. If you have a vintage car, like a '57 Chevy, play Fifties music.

▶ You can't serve alcohol if you're a minor. However, you could offer mock champagne, crystal glasses and a fancy ice bucket.

▶ If you have an unusual or vintage car, decorate it accordingly. For example, if you have an old Chevy, hang dice from the front mirror.

▶ Keep your car *immaculate*, inside and out.

▶ Drop off and pick up your clients directly in front of their destination. Don't let them walk an INCH farther than they have to!

▶ Be ultra-courteous.

▶ For formal dates, offer a flower to the ladies, perhaps a boutonniere for the gentlemen.

▶ Drive safely. Your clients will want to cruise along slowly to savor the experience.

In large cities, chauffeur services run anywhere from $40 to $180 an hour, depending upon the vehicle. You probably won't have access to a stretch limo, so you'll have to charge less. Charge enough to cover your car expenses at 20 to 25 cents per mile, plus earn you at least $5 per hour. That should put you well under your competition.

Other opportunities exist besides just driving for fancy occasions such as dates, dances, anniversaries, and birthdays. Your bread and butter business might come from strictly routine driving around town for people who don't have access to a car. A good market to tap is retirement homes. A visit to the director, plus posters at the retirement facility, might get you regular work. You could schedule a regular pickup and delivery service for shopping or doctor's visits. If you pick up some regular clientele, consider acting as a combination chauffeur and tour guide. You could schedule outings for as many people as your vehicle holds to local places of interest. Another market to tap for people without vehicles might be large apartment complexes. Many occupants of apartments are without cars and could use a regular trip to the laundromat or grocery store.

The best way to advertise is to advertise your vehicle, particularly if it's a really unique machine. Hang a magnetic sign on the side door with your name and phone number advertising your service, and cruise around town regularly. Sign up for every local parade. Place posters in your school. You'll be able to pick up lots of business for dances, especially proms. If you have a vintage car, contact local caterers. They might be able to use your vehicle for theme parties. For example, you could pick up all the guests invited to a Fifties party in your '57 Chevy, or park it in front of the host's door.

Idea
46

General Errand Service

Job Description: Jack-of-all trades: pickup, delivery, shopping, and general errand person

Personal Traits Required: A cheerful disposition and a willingness to help

Experience Required: A good driving record

Materials Required: A reliable vehicle with roomy storage capacity

Marketing Method: Direct sales, newspaper ads, door-to-door flyer

Expected Wages: Around $5 per hour

A general errand boy (now errand person) might seem to be the hallmark of a bygone era. It used to be that all small businesses, banks and professionals kept at least one jack-of-all-trades on the payroll. Having someone around to run errands is just as useful today as yesterday, but there's usually no one available to do it. The freelance "errand person" should be able to pick up lots of small jobs in the community.

What are some services you could offer?

For the business and professional community:

▶ Shopping, especially for office supplies

▶ Pickup and delivery of papers and parcels

▶ Regular delivery of food or snack supplies

▶ Post office runner

▶ Bank runner, to get change or deposit money

▶ Money collection from customers

▶ For a retail store or florist—delivery of goods to customers

▶ For a lawyer—going to the courthouse for document delivery or simple research

▶ For a repair service–pickup and delivery of items needing to be fixed

▶ Grocery delivery

For people in your community:

▶ Grocery shopping service

▶ Laundry/dry cleaning pickup and delivery

▶ Driving small children to and from lessons, day care, soccer games, etc.

▶ Driving people back and forth from meetings, church, hair appointments, etc.

▶ General shopping

The people in your community who will need you the most will be those without cars–primarily the elderly, handicapped and shut-ins. You can find them by contacting retirement homes or churches. Establishing a regular grocery store service could be invaluable. Your customers could give you a grocery list once a week; you could select the merchandise and deliver it.

The best way to tap the small business and professional market would be to make personal calls, walking through your downtown area. Leave information about your service with local businesses. If you find one or two business clients, that may be all you'd need to earn good wages. See if your clients will set you up with a regular work schedule, such as twice a week for after-school hours.

If you can't schedule regular work, such as for a business or retirement home, you'll have to try to sell to as many people as possible to earn a steady income. To be effective, you'll need some sort of message service, such as a pager or answering service, so prospective clients can get in touch with you. Review the communication methods in Idea #43.

How do you charge for this? If you have two or three regular clients, charge them by the hour so that you earn at least $5 per hour plus 20 cents per mile for auto expenses. If you divide your time among several customers, you'll have more expenses, such as the cost of advertising plus your answering service or beeper. So, you'll have to charge more per hour to cover expenses. $10 to $15 seems reasonable for a one-hour errand, like a grocery trip.

Idea
47

Refreshment Wagon

Job Description: Restaurateur on the run

Personal Traits Required: You must have some hustle and good planning skills

Experience Required: None

Materials Required: Basic food and snacks plus serving equipment, such as beverage coolers

Marketing Method: Just be where people are hungry

Expected Wages: Unlimited potential

Here's the ultimate entrepreneurial challenge for someone with good planning skills and some hustle. Your challenge is to show up with food where the big food operators aren't, and where people are hungry. That probably won't be difficult in your community. Any public gathering, parade, Little League game, outdoor flea market, tennis tournament, golf tournament or community picnic usually has throngs of hungry, thirsty people. Your job, should you decide to accept it, is to find out the schedule of all the public gatherings where you might be needed, and plan accordingly.

You can keep your food service simple by just reselling basic snack foods and soft drinks you buy at the grocery store, and doubling their price. Set up a table near the public event or sell out of the back end of your car in a crowded parking lot. Doubling the price of grocery store items won't be out of line with what other food vendors charge, plus you'll be providing a convenience worth paying extra for. You can easily earn $10 an hour by offering ice cold soft drinks on a hot day at a softball tournament. Once you build up your sales volume, you'll probably be able to find a wholesale supplier to sell you food in bulk at low, low prices.

If you want to get fancy, prepare some basic food yourself, such as simple sandwiches or brownies. However, you can probably earn just as much or more by buying ready-made food, even if you must pay full retail price. Here are some ideas for simple fare you can offer without much, if any, advance preparation:

▶ Soft drinks

▶ Lemonade

▶ Ice tea

▶ Juice—get the small cans or paper cartons with straws included

▶ Coffee

▶ Cocoa—powdered instant with hot water will do

▶ Cookies, brownies—prepackaged in individual snack size packages are best, rather than home made

▶ Pure junk food—Ho Hos, Ding Dongs, Twinkies, Moon Pies, etc. Be careful about selling these to small children at events like Little League games. Parents these days would probably prefer more nutritious fare.

▶ Hot dogs—steam heat them at home and keep the dogs hot in a thermos. Offer fresh buns and squirt bottles of mustard and ketchup

▶ Fresh fruit

▶ Chips—presented in individual portions

▶ Nachos—buy cardboard serving containers to cut down on the mess. You can buy the cheese sauce in huge institutional containers and keep it warm in a thermos.

▶ Popcorn

When considering menu items, remember: *The simpler the better.* You can make just as much money on items that don't require advance preparation as you can slaving over a hot stove making things from scratch. Many people prefer to eat commercial products in individual wrappers. They feel such products may be safer than homemade items, which are easy to tamper with. (WARNING: If you do prepare food items in your own kitchen for resale, you'll probably fall under the strict codes of your local health department. Check with your city about regulations covering food vendors, usually under the Department of Public Health, Food Inspection Division.)

Another option for selling food is to buy an ice cream wagon, either the push kind or the kind you pedal like a bicycle. However, this would be good only for the summer months, and would severely limit the merchandise you offer. Some people make a killing by buying a popcorn cart and setting up in a shopping mall. Of course, both of these options require a greater front-end investment than a simple drinks and snacks operation you could run out of your car.

Think about the seasons, and plan your food and drinks around the temperature in your area. In the fall and winter, people like hot beverages and nutritious snacks, such as apples and popcorn. In the summer, ice cold drinks and chips are more in order.

No matter what you will be selling, check city ordinances and with your health inspector before you begin business. Some cities severely restrict or ban small food vendors. Find out if you need a special license or permit. Also, check to see if your sales are subject to any local or state taxes.

You won't need to do any formal advertising. Just show up at community events. There are methods to draw attention to your business while you're there. Put up a large banner with a catchy business name on it. Float a few big, colorful balloons above your car or snack table. Wear a wild hat or costume. If you're serving food at an evening event, find a flashing lantern or spotlight. If it doesn't interfere with the main event, bring some music along, a radio or tape player. Music always draws a crowd.

Ventures for Mail Order

48. Handicrafts/Hobbies

49. Resale

50. Personalized Products

Mail order is the business of selling products that are ordered and delivered through the mail. Modern day mail order now also includes products that can be ordered over the telephone, then shipped by mail. The mail-order business owner never deals with customers face to face. People buy through the mail because it's easy, easier than getting in the car and looking all over town for that certain something. People also order through the mail because mail-order operators offer them products or prices that can't be found in local retail stores.

On the surface, mail order looks like the perfect entrepreneurial venture for a teenager, for the many reasons listed below.

Advantages of a Mail-order Business
1. It's a great part-time business.
2. Your work hours are flexible.

3. It's a relatively low-risk business to start, compared to starting up a retail store or restaurant. You can break in with one or two simple ads in the newspaper or magazines.

4. With proper promotion, you can build up your clientele fast, compared with retail stores that must build slowly.

5. You can make money off your favorite hobbies.

6. You don't need a fancy office or store—just a mailbox!

7. There's no direct selling involved. You don't need to spend time with customers face to face. (Many people consider that a definite advantage!)

However, this section on mail-order ventures is placed at the back of this book for a reason. Mail order is for the few and the brave. It takes more business savvy and sophistication than the other forty-seven ideas. Many people believe that making money in mail order is like taking candy from babies. You simply place an ad in a newspaper or magazine and sit back while the dollars collect in your mailbox. Some ads in the back of reputable magazines seem to promise overnight success in the mail-order business. An ad in a major magazine recently claimed:

> Earn up to $20,000 a month in your spare time in the mail-order business! Learn the secrets of the super rich. Send for my fool-proof guide to setting up your own mail-order business and be on your road to riches. Just $10.95—results guaranteed!

Other problems with the mail-order business are listed below.

Disadvantages of a Mail-order Business
1. Your income is highly unpredictable.

2. Advertising and promotion can be expensive.

3. The business is extremely competitive. If you have a good product, one of the big-time mail-order houses will be quick to copy it.

4. The techniques you choose to promote your products can make or break your business. You can waste a lot of money quickly by advertising in the wrong places.

5. You are subject to very strict federal laws governing the mail-order business. Your ads must be absolutely truthful, or you're subject to prosecution by federal authorities. (You'll notice the example ad copy says "Earn *up to* $20,000 a month . . ." *"UP TO"* means you could earn only 50 cents. In this case, the ad isn't necessarily fraudulent, just misleading.)

There are lots of "secrets" you need to know to set up shop, but these secrets can be found in any number of good books you can find in your library or bookstore. One of the bibles of the mail-order business is:

Julian Simon, *How to Start and Operate a Mail-Order Business* (New York: McGraw-Hill Book Co., 4th edition, 1987)

or its paperback abridged edition by the same publisher:

Getting Into the Mail-Order Business (4th edition, 1984)

Scan your library shelves—there are many other excellent titles available.

All the mail-order guidebooks preach one main message:

There's no such thing as a foolproof, overnight, get-rich-quick scheme in the mail-order business!

No matter how tempting certain ads look, the best way to learn about the business is by doing thorough research, reading, and practicing—*not* by buying a guide through the mail.

The complexities of mail order cannot be covered adequately in this section. This book can give you only some of the basics. Before you take the plunge, be sure to read further.

Getting into Mail Order

No matter what you choose to sell, the process of getting into mail order is basically the same:

I. Select a product or service.
II. Determine your production method.
III. Decide on a promotion strategy.
IV. Determine a price.
V. Develop a communication plan.

I. SELECT A PRODUCT OR SERVICE

First, select a product, group of products or a service that will sell by mail. The product you choose must offer the customer either a significant price advantage over retail, or something unique that can't be found on a local shopping trip. When you select a product, consider the method of shipping. Some items are too bulky, too fragile, too strangely shaped or too dangerous to ship easily through the mail. The beginner shouldn't attempt to mail tropical fish or whipped cream cakes.

II. DETERMINE YOUR PRODUCTION METHOD

If you offer an item you make yourself, you'll need to practice quite a bit to make sure you can produce the item easily in quantities. If you order your products through a supplier, you'll need to locate one that's absolutely reliable. Many mail-order companies don't even order their products in advance of an advertisement. They first place a test ad in a newspaper or magazine, check the response, get the money in from their customers, then place an order with a supplier. Then, they're not risking any of their own money.

III. DECIDE ON A PROMOTION STRATEGY

This third step, deciding how you will promote your product, is the most important step in the mail-order business. There are three basic methods to choose from:

▶ Advertising in newspapers or magazines

▶ Direct mail marketing

▶ Selling to mail-order catalogs

Advertising in newspapers or magazines

This is the classic method of mail-order marketing. However, small ads in national media can cost hundreds, even thousands of dollars. Some recent examples of advertising rates are listed below:

1. National newspaper—*USA Today,* circulation 1.7 million daily (largest circulation newspaper in the U.S.). Ad rates: Classified ad—if you run an ad for three consecutive days, the rate is $26.50 per line per day, with a four-line minimum. For a typical four-line ad, your total bill for three days would be $318.00.
Note: *USA Today* checks out all mail-order products before you advertise. You must mail them a sample of your product and advertisement prior to placing an ad. Once they approve your product, they'll run the ad and return the sample to you.

2. National magazine—*Better Homes and Gardens,* circulation 8 million. Ad rates: $3,010 for their smallest display ad in the mail-order section, 1 inch by 2 and ¼ inches.

3. Regional magazine—*New England Living,* circulation 100,000. A classified ad, size 1⅝ by 2 inches, is $170. Their smallest display ad is 2¼ by 2⅜ inches, at a cost of $365.

4. City newspaper—*The New York Times,* circulation over 1,000,000. Ad rates: Classified section is $11.75 per line per day, with a four-line minimum. $47.00 is their cheapest rate for a one-day ad.

5. Local newspaper—*Danbury News Times,* circulation 40,000. Ad rates: Classified section is $2.25 per day per line, with a four-line minimum. Their cheapest one-day ad is $9.

The above list gives you a cross-section of advertising rates. Rates are based primarily on the numbers of readers a magazine or newspaper has—the fewer the readers, the cheaper the ad rate.

If you want to break into the mail-order business, and you want to hold down advertising expenses, try local or regional shoppers and newspapers first. Or, you could advertise in national magazines with smaller circulation. This works particularly well if you have a very specialized product, such as a needlework kit. Then, just advertise in small circulation magazines whose readers are interested only in handicrafts.

Direct mail marketing

Direct mail means sending letters directly to customers who are likely to buy your products. The cost for direct mail will include the cost for your advertising letter or brochure, plus postage and envelopes—at least thirty cents per customer you are trying to reach. If you want to sell to local churches or businesses, say tire dealers, the best way to market is to look up your target customers in the Yellow Pages. If you want to expand beyond your city, go to the library. They usually stock Yellow Pages from other cities.

If you want to reach individuals or businesses who are likely to be interested in your specific product, on a national or regional level, then you'll need to buy a mailing list. You can find a directory of mail lists in a book called:

Direct Mail List Rates and Data (DMLRD)
(Wilmette, Illinois: Standard Rate and Data Service)

The DMLRD, which is updated semi-annually, can be found in any large library—it's too expensive for you to buy. This directory tells you about all the specialized customer listings you can "rent." You pay a flat fee for one-time usage of a list for direct mail advertising. You'll find specialized lists of all types of customers—from bird lovers to gourmets to stamp collectors to pickle enthusiasts. Prices for lists vary. For example, let's say you invented a great new cake decorating tool. You want to send a direct mail solicitation to people likely to buy your product. A recent DMLRD had the following information:

Quantity	Description	Price per thousand
25,900	Buyers of aluminum cake molds	$15

Thus, the entire list of 25,900 names and addresses would cost you $388.50 to rent one time. Normally, the rental price includes typed, gummed labels to put on your envelopes. As you can see, direct mail marketing is expensive. The choice of the proper list is crucial. If you are considering direct mail marketing, a list broker (who gets a commission from the rental of lists) can give you professional guidance. Look in the Yellow Pages under *Mailing Lists*.

Selling to mail-order catalogs

Another method is to let the pros handle your retail marketing. If you have a very high-quality, unique item, consider selling to national mail-order catalogs such as *The Horchow Collection*. The best way to approach these big companies is to send a very professional cover letter plus a detailed, sharp photograph of your product. The letter should say something about you, your product, and your price. You should state your sales price, whether you offer quantity discounts, plus a suggested retail price for the catalog. (Retail is normally at least twice your sales price to the catalog.) Study the catalog carefully before you send a letter. Your product must be appropriate to the catalog in terms of quality, price and type of merchandise. Your letter should include a brief statement about WHY they should include your product in their catalog. Any mail-order catalog will contain a phone number, usually an "800" toll-free number. Before you send a letter, call first and ask for the catalog purchasing department. Ask for any submission rules they have and who to send your information to, so your letter doesn't get lost or overlooked.

IV. DETERMINE A PRICE

If your product is unique, you'll be able to command a premium price. Your product will probably be unique only until you place that first ad. Then, you'll probably get some competition! Your price needs to cover your production costs, mailing costs, advertising costs, plus earn you at least $4 an hour for your efforts.

V. DEVELOP A COMMUNICATION PLAN

You'll need to decide how to communicate with your prospective customers. Here are a few of the decisions you'll have to make:

1. Will you list your home address in your advertising? Or rent a post office box? Or will you list a telephone number and take orders over the phone?

2. How will you ask for payment? By check, or money order, or credit card? Most mail-order firms use all three. Call a credit card company for their charges and procedures for collecting money for credit card purchases.

3. How will you mail the product to the customer? How can you keep your mailing costs low? How long will it take you to get the product shipped to your customer? (The time it takes to mail to the customer should be listed in your ad. The standard time is four to six weeks.)

One of the complexities of the mail-order business is that it's watched very carefully by the government, both by the U.S. Post Office and the Federal Trade Commission. Why? Many mail-order offers are fraudulent. On any given day in a large city newspaper, there'll be ads for mail-order items that are *completely bogus!* Don't assume that if the newspaper or magazine seems reputable, all the ads are legitimate. There are countless slick operators who put ads in the paper selling items they have no intention of ever shipping. They collect their dollars at a post office box and move around a lot. The government scrutinizes advertising regularly, and investigates complaints by customers who feel they have been cheated by mail-order operators. The government can shut you down, fine you or prosecute you for false advertising, so be wary of how you represent your product in ads. You're not allowed to make exaggerated claims, like "Best widget available on the market," unless you can prove them. Any advertising must be worded carefully. The best way to check your advertising is to let your friends and family read it. What do they think it means? Were they confused, misled or fooled by what you had to say? If so, rewrite the ad. You can get further information about the rules for truthful advertising in almost any good mail-order book, or write to:

The Federal Trade Commission
6 Pennsylvania Avenue N.W.
Washington, DC 20580
Phone (202) 523-1730

Ask the FTC for their Trade Regulation Rule on Mail Order Merchandise or their Weekly News Summary.

Your mail-order business doesn't need to be national in scope to make good money. You can try out ideas for products and advertising locally, and keep your costs way down. It's a safe, cheap way to try out your business ideas before you spend the big money to advertise in the national media.

What are some ideas for products you could sell through the mail? One of the ways to find out is to scan the classified ad sections of national newspapers. Also, check the back of national magazines. This should give you a general picture of what independent operators are selling by mail. If there's a phone number in the ad, you might call the mail-order operator direct. Find out how successful he or she has been, and ask about the response received from advertising. Almost everything under the sun has been marketed by mail. It's your job to separate the golden opportunity from the goose egg.

The following sections will give you some ideas of products that have been successfully marketed by mail. *Warning:* none of the products suggested comes with guarantees of success. Your task will be to select a product wisely – one that you can produce and promote successfully. And, by the way, some of the stories are true. You *can* get rich in mail order. Just don't expect it to happen overnight, without hard work.

Idea

48

Handicrafts/Hobbies

The basics of mail order have already been covered in the preceding pages. This section simply provides a listing of ideas you can pursue for mail order. The advantage of these ideas is that you can make a business out of something you are already doing and (presumably) enjoying.

When you consider making a business out of your handicraft or hobby, don't think you necessarily have to do all the production work. Many people like to buy craft or hobby kits and do the work themselves. You might earn just as much money by selling craft or hobby patterns or instructions, and you can decide whether to include all materials necessary to complete the item.

A good mail-order book from the library or bookstore should contain long lists of craft and hobby ideas. Here are a few ideas for items that have sold well in the past. Remember, in hand-made or hobby items, you need to seek out the *unique* or *different* item.

1. Cooking You can sell individual recipes, recipe books, home-made kitchen accessories, prepared foods that are unique, gourmet ingredients, unique serving or baking dishes, cook's tools, or aprons.

2. Woodworking Kits are quite popular with the do-it-yourself crowd. You provide a pattern and, if it's a small item, the wood and all assembly materials. Some popular kits have been birdhouses, bookracks, keyholders, hatracks, model airplanes, children's toys, umbrella stands or furniture. Small, handpainted, customized pieces are also good sellers.

3. Handicrafts Almost any personalized item is a potential hit. Country decorating accessories are hot right now, too.

4. Ceramics Children's dishes with a handpainted name are popular. Birth announcement plates have always been good sellers. Handpainted anniversary plates or bells have sold well in the past.

5. Costume jewelry

6. Stamps, coins The field of stamps has always been a reliable mail-order moneymaker, but you *really* have to know your stamps, and you'll have a lot of competition. Same with *coins*.

7. Custom artwork Paper silhouettes, photos mounted on canvas or plates, making oil paintings from photos, custom cartooning. You must be a great artist to sell your artwork by mail, and your ad must include a photo of what you're selling.

8. Sewing Curtains, aprons, custom applique work on T-shirts or jogging outfits, Halloween or party costumes, place-mat/napkin sets, tablecloths, quilts, baby linens, doll clothes.

Idea

Resale

This form of mail-order business works well if you locate an *ultra-cheap* supplier of goods, i.e., buy goods directly from a wholesaler and then advertise them for sale through mail order. One way to find products for resale is to find local manufacturers who distribute only locally. In exchange for quantity orders, they might let you order at a deeply discounted price for sale through the mail. One example of this was a sharp operator who hooked up with a small gourmet cheese shop in a small town in Iowa. All the cheese was made and sold locally. The mail-order operator started advertising nationally. As soon as he received an order (the customer had to pay in advance by check), he placed the order with the cheese shop. Therefore, he had no out-of-pocket expenses other than the advertising.

The key to success in resale items for mail order is **PRICE**. You must offer a significant price advantage over what someone could buy the same item for in a retail store. Some examples of successful resale items have been:

▶ Used computer equipment

▶ Pots and pans

▶ Gourmet food

▶ Light bulbs

▶ Home safety devices, such as fire alarms or extinguishers

▶ Wrapping paper assortments

▶ Office supplies

▶ Tools, nails, screws, bolts

▶ State souvenirs—especially for state or regional marketing, such as state mugs, t-shirts, flags

▶ Collegiate souvenirs

▶ Gardener's supplies, such as tools or seeds

▶ Home furnishing accessories

▶ Car washing accessories

▶ Toys

▶ Jewelry—make sure your ads are completely truthful. Don't represent fake gemstones as real.

▶ Clothing, especially novelty items such as fun ties, boxer shorts, T-shirts

▶ Hobbyist accessories. Easier to market than many on this list, because you can find magazines catering to specific hobbies to cut your ad expenses. Woodworking supplies, candy-making equipment, sewing gadgets, etc.

▶ Camping gear

▶ Sports accessories—*cheap* golf balls, tennis balls, etc.

Idea

50

Personalized Products

Probably the best idea in mail order is to invent or discover a unique product. Some say that there's nothing new under the sun. However, you don't have to be an ingenious inventor to market unique products.

Sometimes just offering to personalize a standard, ordinary product used every day by millions could turn into a gold mine. Examples of personalized objects found in mail order include:

Aprons, dishes, spoon rests, book bags, furniture, pencils, stationery, luggage, golf balls, tennis balls, tennis racket covers, clothing, socks, maps, books, diaries, book markers, book covers, school supplies, lunch boxes or sacks, towels, bed linens, mugs, glasses, pillows, eyeglass holders, sunglasses, clothing hooks, bat & ball holders, desk accessories, sneakers, door knockers, door mats, door plaques, mail boxes, jewelry, birthday cards, signs, seat covers, and auto, van or truck accessories.

Another type of unique product is personalized not by name but by town, state, region or school. Flags, pennants, bumper stickers, T-shirts, mugs, hats, salt and pepper shakers, decorative plates, or glasses emblazoned with a state or collegiate motto or humorous phrase could be quite popular. Sometimes, a simple product is the best product. "I'm proud to be from _____" (fill in the blank with your state) with some nice artwork printed on a T-shirt could sell well. If you're from a large city, even a clever city slogan printed on bumper stickers, mugs and shirts could generate a large volume of sales, particularly if your city has a lot of tourist traffic. These items could be sold to the general public via newspaper ads or in regional magazines. Or, you could market directly by letter or sell to retail souvenir or novelty shops. Airport stores are a good candidate for additional sales.

Holiday Ventures

This section is set apart from the other fifty ideas because it can't generate year-round income. However, for those of you who want to pick up some extra cash around holiday time, this section is for you.

The key to making money on holiday ventures is advance planning. You can't jump into a business of Christmas crafts on December 5. You'll need to start planning your products and plotting your marketing strategy at least four months before your hot selling season.

Here are some ideas for holiday money-making schemes, in calendar year order:

New Year's Day

▶ Catering for football games. Offer sandwich trays, meat and cheese trays, hors d'oeuvres, chip and dip platters, glazed hams. You'd be surprised at just how many folks don't feel like cooking on New Year's! The best way to advertise is with a door-to-door flyer in your neighborhood. Ask your customers to place orders at least two weeks in advance, and set a firm delivery time.

Valentine's Day

▶ Sell flowers on the street corner or door to door.

▶ Make artistic Valentine-theme decorations, such as silk floral centerpieces, candle arrangements, party decorations. Sell to boutiques or door-to-door.

▶ Set up a stand on the day before and the day of Valentine's just outside a busy factory parking lot. At closing time, be ready to sell flowers, candy.

St. Patrick's Day

▶ Make humorous badges/buttons proclaiming Irish heritage. Sell to local specialty shops, bars & restaurants.

▶ Make green anythings! Leprechauns, hats, pipes, shamrocks, T-shirts, aprons. Sell door to door, to boutiques or bars.

Easter

▶ Rent an Easter bunny costume and advertise for personal appearances, either door to door or to local merchants and shopping malls.

▶ Make artistic Easter eggs. Sell to boutiques.

▶ Make beautiful centerpieces. Sell at craft fairs, out of your home or door to door.

▶ Hold Easter parties for kids. Charge a flat fee for a two hour session. They can make Easter crafts, hunt eggs, visit with the Easter bunny, etc.

Independence Day

▶ Sell flags of every size door to door.

▶ Sell patriotic decorations for July 4 parties— bunting, streamers, noisemakers, party decorations.

▶ Sell firecrackers or fireworks. (Only if it's legal in your state! Check local regulations.) Set up a booth, or distribute flyers and take orders.

▶ Rent or make an Uncle Sam or Lady Liberty outfit and schedule personal appearances for a fee. Local stores might like you to stand out in front distributing balloons or candy.

Halloween

▶ Make costumes. Many parents don't like the cheap varieties found in most stores at Halloween, the type with the plastic masks. Smaller children don't like to wear masks, either. Fancy department stores and magic shops offer handmade costumes, and charge in the neighborhood of $40 to $60 for a simple clown, witch or fairy. You can buy a pattern from almost any pattern catalog and buy the material. If you offered a well-made costume for $30, you should make at least $5 an hour. This venture takes a lot of advance planning. You can market to specialty shops, costume shops and boutiques. If you do, contact them by midsummer at the latest for an order. Or, you can market door to door in your neighborhood, probably during mid-September. Have samples ready to show, or wear one of your actual costumes. Leave advertising flyers with prospective customers, with descriptions or pictures of the costumes you have. Ask them to place orders with you by the end of September.

▶ Sell pumpkins door to door. Contact a local farmer well in advance to get a cheap deal on his pumpkin harvest, or raise your own. You can offer the plain varity, or a pre-carved "package deal," with a selection of faces available plus a candle already inside.

▶ Make Halloween or harvest-theme decorations. Especially popular are door hangings, but any variety of craft items can be marketed to boutiques or door to door.

▶ Host a children's Halloween party or Halloween craft-making session for a fee. The kids can learn Halloween safety tips, bake cookies and treats, play games or make decorations for their homes.

Thanksgiving

▶ Sell baked goods. Please practice this first! You might specialize in the ever-popular pumpkin pie, or other kinds of pies, cakes, cookies, even pumpkin cheesecake. Sell to local restaurants or door to door, leaving flyers and taking orders in advance.

▶ Make artistic centerpieces, door hangings or decorations with a harvest theme. Market to local boutiques or door to door.

▶ Sell bulk candles at a discount.

▶ Host a children's theme party or craft-making session for a fee. Teach them the story of the pilgrims, make nutritious pumpkin cookies, draw turkeys.

Christmas

▶ There's an endless variety of Christmas crafts. You might want to make these crafts all year long, then go in with friends on a Christmas craft fair. Or, you can sell door to door or rent space at a community crafts fair.

▶ Take advance orders for wreaths and Christmas trees. Find a cheap supplier. Set a delivery date in advance with your customers. Best way to advertise is door to door in your neighborhood.

▶ Sell baked goods, especially beautiful Christmas cookies. Baking Christmas cookies is extremely time-consuming and *expensive!* So, don't price your merchandise too cheaply. Some bakeries charge up to $6 a dozen for Christmas cookies, and they don't even taste homemade. Experiment with several varieties before Christmas and develop an assortment that you find easy to make. Many types freeze well—but be sure to *test* them. Make them in mid-year, freeze them, take them out a month later and try them. Do they still taste fresh? If so, you can gear up your cookie making way in advance of Christmas. You won't have much competition for this, so you should do well. Market your wares door to door, leaving a flyer and taking advance orders around Thanksgiving time. Or, you could probably sell some to local businesses, caterers or restaurants. Cut down your costs by buying all your baking ingredients in bulk and finding attractive but inexpensive containers to wrap the cookies in for delivery.

▶ Rent a Santa costume and make personal appearances for a fee. Advertise in the paper, visit local merchants, or leave a calling card at all your neighbor's houses. You'll need a reliable car (or sleigh!) to drive to your Christmas Eve and Christmas appointments.

▶ Advertise for Christmas party catering or as a party helper. You can simply be available for cleanup and help serving, or offer to make food or plan the entire event.

▶ Host a children's theme party or crafts party for a fee.

▶ Get together a small group of talented singers and an accompanist with a portable keyboard. Sell Christmas caroling to local hotels, shops, even small businesses.

▶ Sell handmade toys, dolls, doll clothing or novelty gift items. Advertise via a flyer, and take advance orders around Thanksgiving time.

▶ Set up a booth or table outside a grocery store or shopping center. (Be sure to ask permission first!) Sell wreaths, candy, crafts, candles. If you live in the South, you can gather live mistletoe from the trees, trim the plants, separate them into small bunches and bag them.

Marketing Tips

All along the way, this book has been sprinkled with marketing tips geared to each specific business venture. This chapter gives you an overview of marketing *promotion*. Promotion is the communications side of marketing – getting the right kind of information out to prospective customers to build your business. Chapter 5 gives examples of promotion tools, from advertising to publicity, and the costs involved.

Marketing promotion is a big subject. Much more is involved than simply taking orders over the phone or selling door to door. It's learning how to attract customers by presenting yourself and your product in the best possible light.

You have four basic promotion "tools" available to help sell your product:

1. Advertising. Any paid form of attracting attention to your business, such as newspaper or magazine advertising.

2. Personal selling. Face-to-face contact with prospective customers, such as selling products door to door.

3. Sales promotion. Incentives designed to draw new customers to your products, such as free coupons or small gift items.

4. Publicity. Free news coverage in the media – information on your business that's reported by the newspaper, TV, magazine or radio.

Advertising

Advertising is the most expensive way of getting your message out to prospective customers, but it can be the most effective. Modern advertising techniques can be quite creative, from skywriting ads over a suburb to renting elephants to parade down Main Street. This section sticks to the more practical and affordable side of advertising suitable to the fifty business ventures in Chapter 4. The following list gives you some basic advertising ideas.

1. Door-to-door flyer Since most of the ventures in this book are meant to be run as neighborhood businesses, the door-to-door flyer will probably be the most effective way to reach your customers. It's also one of the cheapest forms of advertising, and you can afford to put a lot of information in your ads.

Flyers can be hand drawn and photocopied for four to twenty cents per copy, depending upon prices at your local printer. Or, if you have access to a personal computer, you can quickly run off hundreds of copies for less than a penny each. You can also type them and then photocopy the results, or hire a printer to typeset a flyer. The last is the most expensive way to produce flyers, but they look the most professional. Most printers offer flyers on heavy paper (card stock) with holes already punched that fit neatly over doorknobs.

Typical price quote for flyers made by a professional printer:

5½ by 11 inch flyer printed on colored card stock with black printing, with hole cut for doorknob

> Minimum: 100 copies $42, or 42 cents each
>
> 1,000 copies $88, or 8.8 cents each

Add to the per copy price a typesetting fee of $15 to $30

No matter what type of flyer you produce, remember that you can't legally put flyers in mailboxes. The U.S. Post Office allows only stamped mail delivered by one of their carriers. So, flyers must be hand-delivered to your customers' doors. Find a method to attach them to the door so they don't blow away, such as:

▶ Roll up the flyers, using a rubber band to attach them to the doorknob

▶ Tape them to the door

▶ Slip them under the door mat

▶ Punch a slit and a hole just large enough to hang the flyer on the doorknob. (If you do, be sure to leave a blank space on your ad for the hole!)

Flyers give you a lot of room to describe your service. The two things you *can't* forget are your business name and telephone number. Other things to include in your advertising message:

▶ What makes your product unique or special (low price, special features)

▶ What makes you qualified to do the job (awards, good references, experience)

▶ Exact and accurate product or service description (don't exaggerate!)

▶ Why you are better than the competition (faster delivery, more reliable, cheaper, more for the money, you're a neighbor)

If you hand draw your flyer (perfectly fine for neighborhood businesses, as long as the flyers are neat and legible), dress up your ad with a neatly drawn border and some artwork. You can find all kinds of stickers to dress up your flyer at an office supply store—press-on stars, arrows, symbols, punctuation, headline lettering, etc.

Consider other uses for your door-to-door flyers. Many people hand them out or post them at school, church, the grocery store or community events. Or, pin them under the windshield wipers of cars in crowded parking lots. If you will be making personal sales calls to small businesses, take flyers along and leave a copy. Also, you can use them for mailers, mailing them directly to a few, select customers.

Two samples of flyers are shown to give you some ideas.

2. Personal billboard Be your own walking advertisement! When performing your job, or when walking around school or the neighborhood, wear a T-shirt or a hat with your business name and phone number on it. You or any local T-shirt company can iron plain block letters and a phone number on a shirt that prospective customers could see from half a block away. This form of advertising would be particularly helpful for any work you do outdoors. Plus, if you do any door-to-door selling, wearing your business identity on an item of clothing will give you greater credibility. Many people refuse to open their door to a stranger. It helps to dress in some sort of official-looking uniform to gain people's confidence. If you drive, handletter a sign to put on your car, or buy a magnetic sign to hang on your side door. While wearing your T-shirt, talk up your business! If you are selling a product, be sure to have samples ready to show. You can make a point of calling attention to your business by wearing your "personal billboard," your T-shirt or cap, to a crowded place such as a shopping mall on a busy day. Be ready to hand out business cards or flyers so people can contact you later.

Flyer Example 1:

Prepared on a typewriter

```
                  HOLIDAY HOUSE SITTERS

          WANT TO TAKE A WORRY-FREE VACATION
                   OR BUSINESS TRIP

                   RELAX - CALL US!

     HOLIDAY HOUSE SITTERS WILL TAKE CARE OF YOUR
             HOUSE AND LAWN WHILE YOU ARE AWAY

     We provide any or all of the following services:
                   Lawn maintenance
                      Pet care
                     Plant care
                   Daily inspection
              Mail and newspaper pickup
     Turn lights on and off to enhance home security
     Scheduling appointments for delivery or repairmen
       Overnight stays in the house upon request

     DON'T LEAVE YOUR HOUSE EMPTY AND UNPROTECTED!

               CALL HOLIDAY HOUSE SITTERS
        EXCELLENT REFERENCES PROVIDED ON REQUEST
     LET US TAILOR A SPECIAL PROGRAM TO MEET YOUR NEEDS

     LOW, LOW RATES - FREE ESTIMATES

     CALL 438-2000 OR 439-2121 FOR FURTHER INFORMATION
```

Flyer Example 2:

Prepared by a printer

Slit punched for doorknob
fastening

Hole cut for
doorknob

HOUSECARE

A Professional Housecleaning Service
For People Who Have Better Things To Do.
**BONDED • INSURED
TRAINED • DEPENDABLE**
One Time or Regular Service

REASONABLE RATES—GUARANTEED RESULTS

Dial 424-MAID

HOUSECARE   P.O. BOX 1644   PLANO, TEXAS

3. Newspapers Now you're getting into the big bucks. Small town newspapers can be affordable, but ad rates in large cities are extremely expensive. If you live in a metropolitan area and want to do some newspaper advertising, check for neighborhood publications, usually significantly cheaper than the main newspaper. Some communities print "shoppers," newspapers that contain only advertising. A shopper printed and distributed in the Bronx only is going to cost you a lot less than advertising in the *New York Times*.

There are two types of newspaper advertising, classified and display.

▶ **Classified ads** Classified ads are the cheapest for their size. Newspapers lump them together in one section, normally toward the back. You pay by the word or line, and can't do anything fancy with the ad. It's typeset in regular newspaper type size, although some papers offer large, bold-printed headlines. One advantage of classified ads over display is that people looking in a specific section are usually already interested in finding your particular product or service.

▶ **Display ads** Display ads are sprinkled throughout the paper. The smallest display ads are 1 inch by 1 inch, although you can buy a whole page. Display ads give you more flexibility with your advertising format and message. You can use fancy typestyles, art work, even black and white photos. You'll pay extra for those features.

Medium sized city – 100,000 people

Classified ad of four lines	$ 9.00 per day
Display ad 1 inch by 2 inches	$ 28.00 per day

Big city – 1,000,000 people

Classified ad of four lines	$ 36.40 per day
Display ad 1 inch by 2 inches	$275.00 per day

Most newspapers offer a cheaper per day rate if you run your ad by the week or month. Don't expect a one-shot ad to pull in many customers.

4. Business cards Another advertising tool is the business card (sometimes called a calling card). These 2 inch by 3½ inch cards are small, inexpensive, and easy to carry. They give you an extra touch of professionalism, particularly if you will be doing a lot of face-to-face selling. You can pin business cards up everywhere—at grocery stores, community bulletin boards, restaurants. Try using them like "mini-flyers," leaving them tucked into the doors in your neighborhood.

Costs for these cards vary widely, depending upon where you get them printed, the quantity, and how elaborate they are. Some mail order companies advertise 500 plain black and white cards for as low as $8. Typical prices at your local print shop start at $15 per 500, but you can spend quite a bit more than that if you order customized artwork, raised or engraved lettering, more than one color, or special paper such as foil.

5. Posters Posters can be an effective marketing tool, particularly if you are trying to sell a product or service at school. They're easy to make and can be put everywhere—on telephone poles, in the grocery store, along the street, at church, or at community centers. Most grocery stores allow you to put up a poster, but first get permission from the store manager. Two words of caution about using posters. First, your city may have an ordinance banning posters on telephone poles or along the street. Check with authorities before you post any ads in public places. Second, don't put up posters indiscriminately. Think about where the customers are for *your particular business.* Then, put up the posters where your customers will have the highest likelihood of seeing them. For example, if you're selling a birthday party service for small children, a good place to pin up posters is at day care centers.

Just like flyers, you can draw posters by hand, use a typewriter, a personal computer, or a professional printer. See the flyer section for sample costs. You can prepare 8½ by 11 inch flyers, and have them "blown up"—enlarged by a copy machine you can find at your local printer. If you will be putting up posters outside, print your advertisement and take it to a printer who can laminate it, that is, cover it with a protective plastic coating.

6. Give-aways Anyone in the ad promotion business recognizes this term. The give-away is a small gift you leave with prospective customers to keep your name fresh on their minds. To be effective, the give-away needs to be printed with at least your business name and phone number. Check with your local printer, trophy shop or ad promotion company for availability and pricing. Some of the more reasonably priced give-aways are listed below, with sample price quotes. Other inexpensive give-aways include coasters, keyholders, matchbooks, lighters, bookmarks, pens, small flashlights, or desktop pencil holders.

Pencils	Eight cents each and up, depending upon quantity, type, number of letters engraved
Balloons	Ten to twenty cents each, depending upon quantity and printing
Magnets	Twenty to thirty cents each, depending upon quantity, colors, artwork

7. Direct mail If you offer a service or product for small businesses and institutions in your community, the best way to advertise might be direct mail—send potential customers a letter! The easy method is to use a form letter, that is, the same letter sent to every customer, photocopying as many as you need. Or, you can generate "personalized" letters on a personal computer, inserting the prospective customer's name and address on each letter and perhaps a specific greeting (Dear Mr. or Ms. So-and-So). Personalizing the letters on a typewriter will take you much longer than using a form letter. It's not clear whether going to all that bother will get you any more customers than just sending a photocopied form letter.

Basic costs for direct mail will be, of course, the price of a stamp plus stationery expenses. Add to this your cost for photocopying and typing or producing on a computer. Thus, the cost for soliciting just *one* customer will be at least thirty cents, plus your time and trouble.

Direct mail is expensive, and doesn't make sense for every business. Use direct mail for promotion only if you can identify a specific type of customer for your product, and can easily find names and addresses for mailing. A good example is if you want to market newsletters prepared on your word processor. You think that churches and day care centers are likely customers. It's easy to look in the Yellow Pages to find them. If you want to get more serious about direct mail marketing, review the information in *Ventures for Mail Order*.

Many Chamber of Commerce organizations sell mailing lists for their community printed on gummed labels. Some of the larger Chambers have specialized lists, such as a list of all new people who have just moved into the community. All you have to do is buy these pre-printed labels, peel them off, stick them on envelopes, insert a letter and GO! A recent example of a Chamber of Commerce price for a Newcomer's List in a medium-sized town of 100,000 was $7.50 per week. You can choose to buy one week's worth, or every week.

Personal Selling

Some of the ideas in this book don't require much personal selling, direct face-to-face contact with prospective customers. For example, the house-cleaning business or laundry service only requires a handful of clients to earn good money. Books by the hundreds have been written about personal selling—the psychology of sales, how to convince customers, how to close a sale. If you sell products directly to the public, your success will be *directly dependent* on how effective you are at personal selling. Unlike advertising, good personal selling doesn't cost any money. It just takes your time, effort and practice to develop good people skills. Below are a few simple tips on effective personal selling. Pick up a book at the library if you want to delve more deeply into the subject.

1. Develop contacts Talk about your business to everyone you know, even if a person isn't an immediate candidate for your product. At some later date, he or she may recommend you to someone who needs your product or service. Enlarge your circle of friends and acquaintances by joining clubs or service organizations. Talk to the grownups you know at church or synagogue. You may be eligible to join a local chapter of a business or civic organization, such as Toastmasters or the Chamber of Commerce, or at least sit in on meetings. The contacts you develop there can prove to be invaluable. Ask your friends and family to get the word out on your business. Give them posters or business cards to circulate at work or to their friends.

2. Learn to listen When talking with a prospective client, learn to listen. Ask people questions about what they *need*, rather than just telling them what you provide. Always start with a friendly, relaxed greeting. While making your sales pitch, pause now and then to ask people's opinion. If you ask, be sure to *stop* and *listen!*

3. Door-to-door canvassing in your neighborhood Here are some special tips for selling door to door in your neighborhood.

▶ Sell when you're likely to catch people at home. Try early evening (before dark), or on weekends. Avoid the dinner hour; people get annoyed if disturbed while eating.

▶ Dress up, or better yet, wear a T-shirt with your business name on it. People are reluctant to open the door to a stranger. You'll have a much higher success rate if you look great than if you appear scruffy, dirty, or without a shirt wearing ragged cut-offs.

▶ If no one is home, leave a flyer or business card with your business information on it so people can contact you later.

▶ Be fully prepared with a quick, one-minute verbal description of who you are and what you're selling. Don't waste people's time with a long, rambling speech. Look them straight in the eye while you are speaking. A quick, punchy, enthusiastic sales pitch will get your foot in the door.

▶ Leave *something* containing business information with prospective customers, such as a flyer describing your product or service. Then, if people want to think about it, they can contact you later. Or, they may refer your telephone number to a friend.

▶ Be ready to provide references.

4. Selling to businesses or institutional clients If you want to sell a product or service to a small business, school, or community institution, you'll need to have a very polished sales approach. Here are some tips:

▶ Be sure to have samples of your products ready to show, in a professional-looking portfolio or briefcase.

▶ You should have a lengthier sales pitch than you would need for door-to-door selling. Prepare at least a five minute speech. Practice until you know it by heart. Make sure you can deliver it in a relaxed manner. You don't want to sound like a robot.

▶ If you are selling to businesses, dress professionally, like one of your customers. If you will be calling on offices, wear a suit. If you will be calling on construction foremen, dress neatly but casually.

▶ Visual aids can really help your sales pitch. Carry samples, pictures, or posters that can describe or explain your product or service. It will be easier for your clients to remember what you have to say if you have illustrations to accompany your speech.

▶ Keep a price list with you at all times, and be ready to quote prices.

▶ Take a professional-looking flyer or business card to leave with customers, so they can contact you later.

▶ Follow up with one or more friendly phone calls.

Sales Promotion

Sales promotion means offering discounts, prizes, free gifts, gimmicks, special deals, one-time-only introductory prices and other incentives to attract new customers. Promotions usually don't involve much, if any, out-of-pocket expense, but they will cut into your income. The purpose of sales promotion is to call attention to your product and get someone to buy NOW! Here are some examples of sales promotion methods you can use for businesses in this book:

1. Introductory price Offer a lower than normal price to attract first-time customers. This is particularly useful for a service business. You can circulate door-to-door flyers with a fifty–percent–off coupon for a first-time trial.

2. Free gifts Present a free gift along with purchase of your service or product. For example, you could offer a free bottle of vinyl cleaner to people who buy your car wash service, or throw in a car wax to first-time buyers.

3. Coupons Offer a coupon that discounts the first purchase, or discounts the *next* purchase. For example, you could offer a twenty-five-percent-off coupon for a first time house clean, or do the first one for regular price, offering the *second* clean for twenty-five percent off.

4. Free trials or samples Simply *give away* a small (very small) portion of your service or product. For example, you could offer to clean just *one* window to demonstrate your cleaning ability.

5. Prizes This is a popular incentive offered by many businesses, large and small. Purchase of your product or service entitles your customer to register in a contest to win a prize. For example, if you are repairing bicycles, you could offer a bike radio as a prize to be given away at a set date in the future. Ask your customers to fill out small forms with their name and phone number so you can contact them later. Store forms in a box and pick a winner on contest award day. The advantage of registering customers is that you have a permanent record of names and telephone numbers that you can use later to contact for special deals.

6. Gimmicks A sales promotion "gimmick' is any ingenious or novel device that draws attention to your business and pulls in customers. For example, offer to donate $1 for each swimming pool you clean to the Red Cross or American Heart Association. Give "Good Citizen" plaques to your recycling customers as a thank you for helping you and your environment.

7. Incentives You can appeal to your customers' basic greed by offering them money or discounts for selling your service to their friends or neighbors. This is another very popular sales promotion technique. For example, if customers sign up a neighbor for a long-term housecleaning service, they get one housecleaning for free–or at half price.

Publicity and Public Relations

This is a form of marketing promotion that many small businesses overlook. Publicity is the flip side of advertising. Advertising requires you to PAY to get in the media–the newspaper, magazines, radio or TV. Publicity produces *free* coverage by the media. Big companies often keep a large staff whose sole job is to get free media coverage.

There are two ways you can try to get free coverage by the news media: 1) by issuing press releases or 2) by staging media "events" or "happenings." Some small companies hire a public relations firm or free-lance publicist to get the word out on their business. You won't be able to afford high professional public relations fees. The good news is–it's quite simple to do your own basic publicity work.

1. The Press Release (sometimes called a news release)

A press release is simply a statement that *you* prepare describing your business. It should include anything newsworthy, unique or different about you, your product or service. After you prepare a good press release, send it to all the local or regional media: newspapers, radio stations, TV stations, magazines, and influential people. Just your age and ambition in starting a business might be newsworthy enough to get you coverage. For example, a fourteen-year-old Dallas boy who started his own window-washing company was interviewed on the 6:00 p.m. news on Dallas' most-watched TV station. Over 170,000 people watched the boy tell about his service. This two-minute interview cost the boy nothing. If he had paid for a TV advertisement during the same time slot, it would have cost thousands of dollars.

Here are the few basic rules in preparing a press release:

▶ It should be typed, double-spaced, with wide margins, on 8½ by 11 inch plain white paper.

▶ It shouldn't be more than one page in length.

▶ The standard format is:

Your company name across the top
A contact name (probably you) with a **phone number**
A suggested release date
A catchy headline
Your town and state
Your message
Today's date

See the example on the next page. The release date is usually "FOR IMMEDIATE RELEASE," unless you want the article held for publication until a later date. It's best to send the article in while it's "hot"—ready for immediate publication.

▶ The headline should be an eye-catcher—interesting, informative. It's *supposed* to be news.

▶ Put the most important information in the first paragraph, the least important in the last paragraph. If the media wants to print a shortened version of your release, they usually cut from the bottom. Read through your message and ask yourself: Can the first paragraph stand alone? Does it tell the entire story? If it doesn't, rewrite. The first paragraph should contain the *who, what, why, where* and *when* of your business.

▶ Make an extra effort to write your message in an interesting way. If it's dull and boring, no one will read it and no one will print it. Most newspapers are flooded with hundreds of press releases. The majority are tossed in the wastebasket. Yours *has* to stand out. Think of a special angle to make it newsworthy. Add humor, tie it to some important community event, use names of well-known people (if appropriate), add an element of mystery or tragedy. See the following sample press release.

Sample Press Release

The Carlisle Pride Company
246 Oaklawn Avenue
Carlisle, West Virginia

CONTACT: Jacey Morris, President
Telephone: (999) 555-4567

FOR IMMEDIATE RELEASE

MAYOR PROCLAIMS CARLISLE STUDENT TOWN'S BIGGEST BOOSTER!

CARLISLE, WEST VIRGINIA—Jacey Morris, 15-year-old president of Carlisle High School's Honor Society, has started up a new venture, The Carlisle Pride Company, to boost Carlisle's flagging spirits. Morris, called by Mayor Bob Thomas "the town's biggest booster," offers a complete line of products designed to renew community pride. T-shirts, bumper stickers, mugs, pennants, even baby clothes have been printed to proclaim the new city slogan endorsed by the City Council—"CARLISLE WE LOVE YOU!" Morris will be offering his novelty items for sale in local drug and grocery stores, or can be contacted directly at his home phone (999) 555-4567 to place an order.

Morris dreamed up the idea while the city was recovering from the worst flood in its history. "Everyone I talked to after the flood seemed so depressed. Carlisle is a great town. We can't let this get us down," says Morris. "I wanted to do something for the citizens of Carlisle to lift their spirits. Wearing one of these shirts, or putting bumper stickers on cars will let everyone else know we're proud to be from Carlisle."

6/18/90

2. Staging media events Another way to get free media coverage is to stage a newsworthy "event" or "happening." This is an old gimmick that many small businesses have used. Plan an event, and tip the local media off with a phone call, press release or letter before the event is to take place. Then send out another press release after the event to tell the media how successful it was. Some examples geared to business ideas in this book are listed below:

▶ Idea #1, **Auto Detailing**
Organize a free car wash in a busy parking lot. Prop up a large poster or billboard people can read from their cars as they drive by, and pass out your business cards. Be SURE your phone number is on the poster.

▶ Idea #4, **Neighborhood Directory**
Organize a neighborhood picnic, potluck style, at your home or a local park. Discuss your directory and pass out flyers.

▶ Idea #12, **Lawn Service**
Sponsor a "lawn of the month" contest in your neighborhood for the nicest-looking yard. Put a sign in the yard of the winner for thirty days (with their permission) and/or give a small prize.

▶ Idea #31, **Clowning Around**
Donate some time to charity, making public appearances at a children's hospital or retirement home.

▶ Idea #45, **Chauffeur Service**
Decorate your car with balloons, banners, streamers. Dress up in a great costume, tux or uniform. Park on a busy street corner or parking lot and pass out business cards or give a free spin around the block.

6

Bookkeeping and Accounting Guidelines

Bookkeeping – keeping track of your financial records – is often the biggest area of concern for small business owners. It needn't be. Many people view bookkeeping as the most exciting part of their business. Good records give you an instant business scorecard, to see how well you're doing and to watch your profits grow. Bookkeeping doesn't *have* to be complicated or time-consuming. You *can* do it yourself! It just requires taking time out on a *regular* basis to keep track of income and expenses. For the small businesses described in this book, bookkeeping shouldn't take more than thirty minutes to an hour every week.

There are two basic reasons for keeping good business records. *First,* it gives a picture of how a business is doing, whether you're earning a profit or taking a loss. Sometimes, in the flurry of writing a lot of checks to pay for business expenses and collecting money from customers, you lose sight of whether or not you're earning a profit. SECOND, the government says that you *must* keep track of all your expenses and income for tax purposes. How you choose to do that is up to you. If all your financial records are kept on the back of green envelopes, but they're filed neatly, you've fulfilled the government's basic requirements.

You *don't* need to be an accountant to keep adequate records. Taking a bookkeeping course in high school or a local community college will certainly help, but it's not absolutely required. Hiring an accountant can help, but the fees are high. You can learn to do the basic bookkeeping required for your own business.

You *don't* need a computer to keep your records. You DON'T need to use fancy accounting systems. A simple recording of all the money spent and earned will do the job. Sounds easy, right? The only thing you DO need to be careful of is to write everything down promptly, and keep receipts for items you buy.

The *best* way to keep records is to go to an office supply store and buy a bookkeeping "system." There are many inexpensive recordkeeping books for small businesses; however, this is one area where you don't want to cut corners. The inexpensive bookkeeping systems costing less than $8 don't provide much help. Spend the extra few dollars and invest in a complete bookkeeping record system. The best one available on the market today for the small business owner is the IDEAL Bookkeeping and Tax Record. It comes in a sturdy 9½ by 12 inch plastic binder; the current price is around $28. The IDEAL system is available for twelve different types of businesses, from farming to beauticians. If you are in a service business that does *not* sell products, you'll probably want the PROFESSIONAL SERVICE BOOKKEEPING & TAX RECORD. If you plan on selling wholesale or retail products, you'll need a GENERAL BUSINESS or a RETAIL SALES version. What's great about the IDEAL system is that it explains virtually everything in easy-to-understand language. It's so well organized that it practically does your work for you. The IDEAL System contains separate sections to keep track of income, expenses, bank transactions, payroll, money you owe (accounts payable) and money owed to you (accounts receivable). Each section begins with clear instructions on accounting rules and has one page of filled-out examples.

The rest of this chapter contains brief descriptions of the types of accounts you'll need for a small business. You probably won't need all of them, but scan through each section for the ones relevant to the business you've selected. If you have further questions, look through the pages of the bookkeeping system you purchase, find a good bookkeeping guide for small business at the library, or contact your local Small Business Administration office or IRS. Types of accounts listed in this chapter are:

1. Income
2. Expenses
3. Bank Account/Cash
4. Accounts Receivable
5. Accounts Payable
6. Assets
7. Depreciation
8. Inventory
9. Payroll

Basic Bookkeeping for a Service Business

Most of the fifty ideas in this book are basic service businesses—just *you* selling your own time and expertise. This section describes how to keep records for a service business.

It assumes you:

▶ *Don't* have employees

▶ *Don't* make or buy products for resale

▶ *Don't* buy any expensive equipment that has a useful life of more than one year (called an *asset,* which we'll cover later)

▶ *Get paid* for your work when you actually do the work. In other words, your customers pay you now, not later.

▶ *Pay for* all your materials and supplies when you receive them, in other words, you don't buy on credit

The above items can make your recordkeeping more complicated; these special cases will be covered later in this chapter.

For a simple service business, the only types of records to keep track of are:

▶ Income

▶ Expenses

▶ Bank Account/Cash

1. Income is money received for your services (sometimes called revenue or earnings). In your bookkeeping records, keep track of all money received from customers under *income,* with the date received and a check number if the customer pays by bank check.

2. Expenses are all the costs to run your business. Some examples of *expenses* are:

Office supplies	Car expenses
Telephone bills	Postage
Work supplies	Uniforms
Advertising	

Important note: Your own labor is *not* an expense. You cannot include a *"per hour"* charge for your labor as a business expense.

The best way to keep track of *expenses* is to open a bank account and pay for everything by check, not cash. For each *expense* item, write down the check number, to whom paid, the amount and the date in your bookkeeping record. The cancelled check from the bank gives an additional backup record for the government. Ask for receipts for everything you buy, and keep them filed by calendar date. The IDEAL System allows you to organize *expenses* by category, with a separate column for such *expense* items as office supplies, materials, etc. This is helpful in tracking specific costs.

If you use a car for business, you can keep track of your automobile expenses in two ways:

▶ **Actual Cost** Keep track of all actual expenses such as gas, oil, tires, and repairs. Deduct a *percentage* of these expenses, in the same percentage you use the car in your work. For example, if you use the car 50 percent for work and the other 50 percent for basic transportation to school, you can only claim 50 percent of the expense as a business cost.

▶ **Allowable Mileage** Another way the government allows you to keep track of car expense is simply to record your actual business mileage. Then, they let you use a standard cost per mile as a business expense. In 1989, the government standard was 25½ cents per mile. So, if you drove 600 miles during the year on business, deduct $153 for car expenses (600 × .255). You can choose to make an entry to record car expenses on the *per mile* basis every day, week, month, or at the end of the year.

The government allows either method. If your actual auto expenses were *higher* than the 25½ cents allowance (for example, if you had high repair bills), then you can choose to use actual cost rather than the 25½ cent rate. If you use the *actual cost* method, you *must* keep accurate records of all expenses.

3. Bank Account/Cash Besides *income* and *expenses,* you'll need to keep track of all bank transactions—withdrawals and deposits. This way, you keep track of everything twice, providing an extra check on the bookkeeping records. You'll make an entry into the bookkeeping records under *income* for each customer who pays you. You'll also make an entry in the *bank account* section when you actually put that money in the bank. The *bank account* section looks like the record sheet in the back of any bank book. It gives you a picture of how much cash is on hand. At the end of the month, the bank mails you a statement. You'll have to *reconcile* this bank statement to your bookkeeping records, making sure they agree. Otherwise, either you or your bank has made a bookkeeping error. You'll have to find it and fix it.

Important note: As the owner of a small business, from time to time you may need to invest some money of your own in the business, depositing cash into your bank account. This isn't counted as *income. Income* comes only from customers. When you deposit your own money in your business account, you make a note of the entry in your *bank account* section as a *"capital investment,"* with the amount of money and date. Likewise, it's perfectly OK to withdraw money from your bank for your own personal use. This is *not* an *expense!* It's not really considered *pay,* either. Record personal withdrawals in your *bank account* section as *"owner's withdrawal,"* with the amount and date. Many bookkeeping systems include a special section to keep track of owner's capital investments and personal withdrawals in a section called *"proprietor's account."* Even if your bookkeeping system has a separate section, you'll still need to record the entries under *bank account* to keep the bank account balanced.

Minor Complications

OK! We've discussed the three basic types of records required in a service business—*income, expenses,* and *bank account/cash.* Some of the business ideas in this book require some additional accounts, described below. Run through this checklist to see if you'll need any of them.

▶ **Will you let some of your customers pay later?**

If so, you'll need to keep an *accounts receivable* record. See Item no. 4 below.

▶ **Will some of your suppliers let you buy on credit?**

(In other words, will you receive merchandise and pay later?) If so, you'll need to keep an *accounts payable* record. See Item no. 5 below.

▶ **Will you make any major investments in expensive equipment that lasts longer than one year?**

(Such as a computer, car, desk, paint sprayer.) If so, you'll need to keep a record of *assets* and *depreciation.* See Items no. 6 and no. 7 below.

▶ **Will you make or buy products for resale, either on a wholesale basis or directly to the public?**

You'll need to do some *inventory accounting.* See Item no. 8 below.

▶ **Will you have employees working directly for you on a regular basis?**

If so, you'll need to keep *payroll* records. See Item no. 9 below.

4. Accounts Receivable records track customers who owe you money. If you work for someone and don't get paid right away, then don't record the payment due under *income.* Record it under *accounts receivable!* If you demand and receive payment immediately upon performing your work, you won't need to keep an *accounts receivable* record. The best policy is to ask for cash (or check, of course)! If you have customers in your *accounts receivable* section, as soon as they *do* pay, record their payment as *income.*

5. Accounts Payable This is where you track materials you have bought and received but have not paid for yet–in other words, things purchased on credit. You probably won't need to keep *accounts payable* records, because most small businesses pay for everything the day of purchase. Only large companies with good credit ratings qualify to buy things on credit. Also, by paying for everything the day you buy it, you'll simplify your recordkeeping. If you purchase something on credit, record it under *accounts payable.* On the day you actually pay the bill, then record it under *expense.*

6. Assets, and **7. Depreciation** are two types of accounting records that go hand in hand. *Assets* are major business purchases that last longer than one year. Examples of *assets* are furniture, a computer, typewriter, or a telephone answering machine. (*Expenses* are things that are used immediately or in less than one year's time, such as telephone bills or office supplies.) You can't claim 100 percent of the cost of an *asset* in the year you buy the item if you will be using that item over a long term.

The government has rules about how to keep track of *assets.* Every *asset* has a number of years the government says it will last. For example, personal computers are supposed to last five years. Thus, the first year in business, you can use only one-fifth of the original cost of the computer as a business expense. The annual portion of the *asset* used as a business expense is called *depreciation. Depreciation* is supposed to represent the actual wear and tear on equipment that lasts longer than one year. You can *depreciate* new or used equipment. If you buy new equipment, base the depreciation upon the actual cost of the equipment and keep the original receipt. If you have used equipment, base *depreciation* on actual cost or *fair market value.* Let's say you've had an old desk in your room for ten years. It's perfectly *ok* to deduct a portion of its value as a business expense if you use it *only* for business. Let's say you have no idea how much the desk cost when it was new. You'll need to establish a *fair market value* for it. A reasonable value could be $100 if it's a nice desk. Furniture is supposed to last 15 years. Therefore, you deduct $100 divided by $15, or $6.66 as a *depreciation* expense every year.

If *depreciation* sounds tricky, your bookkeeping system will have some examples, or call the U.S. Internal Revenue Service. They'll be glad to help. Their hot line for all tax and recordkeeping questions is: 1-800-424-1040. It's a free call. Or, ask them for their IRS Publication #534, called *Depreciation.* IRS advice is always free, and for most basic questions, they can give an answer that's just as good as one from an expensive accountant.

8. Inventory If you make or buy products for resale, such as in the mail-order business, you'll need to do some *inventory* accounting. *Inventory* is the amount of unsold goods you have on hand at the end of the year. You need to worry about *inventory* only at the end of the year. Why? Because as you buy materials or products during the year, you'll record their cost under the *expense* section, not in a separate *inventory* section. However, at the end of the year, to calculate *profit* accurately and pay the right amount of taxes, you'll have to deduct the value of *inventory* from total *expenses.* You haven't sold your products in *inventory,* so you haven't earned the *income* for them yet. If you haven't earned the *income,* you can't claim the related *expenses* as a tax deduction.

Of all the accounting described in this chapter, *inventory* is the most complicated. If you have a large *inventory* left at the end of the year, it's best to get some professional accounting advice or read up on *inventory* accounting. If your *inventory* is worth less than $500, the IRS won't mind a close estimate rather than a sophisticated accounting method. Keep in mind that you don't need *inventory* accounting for a simple service business. Items that you use in your regular work that you *don't* sell to customers, such as cleaning supplies used for house cleaning, do not count as *inventory.* Below is a simple example of what happens to the value of your *inventory* at the end of the year.

Example
Molly's Beautiful Bears
Income Statement for the Year Ending December 31, 199__

Revenue on sale of 1,000 stuffed bears @ $8 each $8,000

Less:

Business expenses   (car, office, telephone, etc.)   (500)

Cost of goods sold   (materials and supplies to make 1,100 bears @ $4 each)   (4,400)

Subtotal		**$3,100**
Add back in:	Year-End Inventory	
	(100 bears @ $4)	400
Total Profit		**$3,500**

In this case, Molly sold only 1,000 bears. She made 1,100 bears. To calculate her profit, she needs to add back in her cost of goods for the 100 bears left in *inventory* at the end of the year. She'll earn the profits and claim the costs for those bears next year.

9. Payroll This book strongly advises against hiring employees because of the red tape and extra bookkeeping requirements. Employees are people you hire, manage and control—who work regularly under your direct supervision. The ideas in this book don't require employees. If you pay someone to help you with your business, such as a professional accountant or kids to distribute door-to-door flyers for one or two days, they aren't technically your employees. You simply write them a check for their "professional fees," and record the amount under *expenses,* rather than *payroll.* Payroll recordkeeping makes book work much more complicated. The IDEAL system walks you through detailed examples of payroll accounting if you feel you need help.

The Income Statement
The various types of accounts discussed in this chapter are like pieces of a puzzle. You'll want to see what that puzzle looks like all put together. When you summarize your records, the results are called an *income statement.* An *income statement* is prepared regularly to check business progress, to see how you're doing, to check if you're actually earning a profit. It's also used to prepare quarterly or yearly tax statements. (See Chapter 7 for tax information.)

The IDEAL System explains in detail how to summarize records in an *income statement,* and gives a clear picture of what it should look like. This income statement can be prepared daily, monthly, quarterly or yearly. It's primarily for your own information, to use in managing your business. It comes in handy when talking to a banker about applying for a bank account or loan, or showing to your parents so they'll know how well you're doing. An example *income statement* is included on the next page. You can prepare your own using the example, or use the forms in your recordkeeping system book.

Example

Income Statement
Pete's Executive Auto Detailing

Statement of Income
For the Month Ending January 31, 199__

Income

From basic auto detailing	$600	
From sale of products	350	
TOTAL INCOME		$950

Less: Expenses

Materials used in auto detailing	($ 30)	
Products bought for resale	(250)	
Total expenses		($280)

Profit $670

(*Note:* During this year, Pete bought and sold products to his customers, but at the end of the year he didn't have any extra products on hand, so he doesn't need any *inventory* accounting.)

Calculation of dollars earned per hour

Total hours worked:

30 cars @ 2 hours per car	60 hours
Marketing time (delivering flyers)	5 hours
Administrative time (answering phone, buying products, keeping books)	15 hours

Total hours worked 80 hours

$670 profit divided by
80 total hours worked = $8.38 per hour

(*Note:* This income statement is for example purposes only. It's not necessary for an income statement to include an estimate of dollars earned per hour, but it's good information for you to know.)

$$\boxed{7}$$

Government Reporting Requirements and Tax Information

Government forms and taxes often give the most seasoned business owners heartburn. This chapter is designed to set your worries at ease, and separate fact from fiction.

Fiction: The government doesn't care about a teenager's income, and won't ever find out about mine. None of my friends pay tax, so why should I?
Fact: A self-employed person earning more than $400 per year must pay Self-Employment Tax (Social Security Tax) to the government.
Fact: The government *can* find out about you—through bank records, through examining your customer's bills. They *can* prosecute you for not paying your tax!

Fiction: It's *ok* to lump my income in with my parents'. Who cares, right? Money is money.
Fact: *If* you are self-employed, in other words, if you run a small business, *and*

If you earn more than $400 per year, you *must* file your own 1040 Tax Return separate from your parents.

Fiction: If I earn a lot of money on my own, my parents can no longer claim me as a dependent on their own 1040 Tax Return.
Fact: If you are a full-time student and your parents contribute more than half of your living expenses, you can still be claimed as a dependent *no matter how much you earn!* There was an important tax change in 1987, which affects all tax returns filed since 1988. In previous years, for full-time students, *both* the parents and the student could claim a deduction for the student as long as parents were providing at least fifty percent of that student's support. Now, only one deduction is allowed, and that is on your parents' return.

Fiction: If I run a part-time garage sale service, I don't need to pay state sales tax. Nobody really cares about a small potato operation run by a kid.

Fact: Most states require that you keep records and collect sales tax for *any* sale of merchandise, new or used, to the public. You might be subject to large fines if you don't. Pleading ignorance of the law is never an excuse to avoid paying taxes or fines if you are caught. Check with your state about sales tax laws.

Fiction: I'll need to hire an expensive tax accountant to prepare my tax return.

Fact: A small business proprietor normally needs to fill out only four pages of tax forms:

▶ 2 pages for the basic **1040 U. S. Individual Income Tax Return**

▶ **Schedule C:** Profit or (Loss) from Business or Profession

▶ **Schedule SE:** Self-Employment Tax (Social Security Tax)

If you've maintained good bookkeeping records all year, you should be able to fill out a tax return.

Chapter 3 of this book discusses all the reporting requirements necessary to start up your business. You might want to go back and review that section again. This chapter will stick to the actual reporting required for the federal government and show you how to fill out forms once your business is rolling.

This chapter does not cover state, county or city reporting requirements. Rules and forms vary drastically from one part of the country to the other, and can't be covered adequately here. Chapter 3 describes what reporting and tax requirements you might be subject to in your area. Always check with local authorities before starting a business to determine your obligations for business reporting and taxes.

Federal Government Requirements

You have two basic reporting obligations for the U.S. government:

▶ Income Tax reporting

▶ Self-Employment Tax (Social Security Tax) reporting

Before diving into the subject of federal tax reporting, there's one very important thing to remember:

The Internal Revenue Service (IRS) is there to help you, the taxpayer, fill out your tax forms, *believe it or not!*

If you have questions about tax or business recordkeeping, call the IRS hotline at 1-800-424-1040. It's a free service. If you need general assistance in preparing a tax return, you can go to any local IRS office and meet with an IRS representative. IRS taxpayer service personnel are perfectly willing to sit down and go over your return, because that's their job. Again, this service is provided *free of charge.* Many people are reluctant to approach the IRS for help, for fear the government will uncover something in their records that's wrong, shady or illegal. *Don't worry about that!* IRS taxpayer service representatives aren't out to get you. They sincerely want to help. No question is too stupid, too trivial for them. If they uncover a problem in the way you're keeping records, they'll help you fix it, not turn you in to the Feds.

Another service the IRS provides is free information. You can call the national IRS hotline or your local office to receive free pamphlets, shipped in two weeks or less. IRS publications you might want to read are:

#334	Tax Guide for Small Business
#533	Self-Employment Tax
#534	Depreciation
#535	Business Expenses
#551	Basis of Assets
#583	Information for Business Taxpayers— Business Taxes, Identification Numbers, Recordkeeping

Tax Return Preparation

This section demonstrates how to fill out an actual tax return. Before looking at tax forms, here are a few matters of importance to remember:

▶ As a sole proprietor, your income is the same as the income from your business. You don't need to fill out two returns, one for you and one for your business. Essentially, your business has *no* income—it all goes to you. Therefore, you don't pay income tax rates for business, you pay *personal* income tax rates.

▶ Your income is simply all your revenue, less your expenses. You can't include your own labor expenses as a cost of doing business.

▶ You pay two types of tax: income and self-employment tax. However, you file and pay both taxes at the same time.

▶ Tax laws change every single year! Rules change, tax rates change, forms change. The forms in this book are current through 1990, but check with the latest IRS publications for updates.

Following this section is a sample tax return, filled out using Idea #21, House Cleaning, as an example. The tax return has four parts:

▶ 1040 U.S. Individual Income Tax Return – Page One

▶ 1040 U.S. Individual Income Tax Return – Page Two

▶ Schedule C: Profit or Loss From Business

▶ Schedule SE: Social Security Self-Employment Tax

Housecare, the name of the business used in this example, doesn't have any assets (large-scale equipment with a useful life of longer than one year). If you use assets in your business, you'll also need to fill out Form 4562, Depreciation and Amortization, and include it with your tax return.

In the return used as an example, Amanda J. Keller has

	$3400 in **income**
minus:	$223 in **expenses**
equals:	$3177 in **profit,** or **adjusted gross income**
deducting:	$3100 as a standard deduction
equals:	$77 in total **taxable income**
She owes:	$13 in **income tax**

Notice that after subtracting her standard deduction, she owes $13 in personal income tax. Amanda also owes $414 in Self-Employment Tax, which is reported on Schedule SE, Social Security Self-Employment Tax. Therefore, her total tax bill for the year is $427. (*Note:* All calculations and examples are based upon tax rates and forms current through December 31, 1990.)

If you have any specific questions about the tax return examples or how they relate to you and your business, consult IRS Publication 334, a 185-page Tax Guide for Small Business, or ask your local IRS office.

Form **1040**	Department of the Treasury—Internal Revenue Service **U.S. Individual Income Tax Return**	**1989** (B)			OMB No. 1545-0074

For the year Jan.–Dec. 31, 1989, or other tax year beginning , 1989, ending , 19

Label
Use IRS label.
Otherwise,
please print
or type.

Your first name and initial **Amanda J.** Last name **Keller**

Your social security number **483 123 4567**

Spouse's social security number

Home address (number and street). (If a P.O. box, see page 7 of Instructions.) **#20 Oak Grove** Apt. no

City, town or post office, state and ZIP code. (If a foreign address, see page 7.) **Decatur, IL 01234**

For Privacy Act and Paperwork Reduction Act Notice, see Instructions.

Presidential Election Campaign ▶
Do you want $1 to go to this fund? ✔ Yes ☐ No
If joint return, does your spouse want $1 to go to this fund? ☐ Yes ☐ No
Note: Checking "Yes" will not change your tax or reduce your refund.

Filing Status
Check only one box.
1 ✔ Single
2 ☐ Married filing joint return (even if only one had income)
3 ☐ Married filing separate return. Enter spouse's social security no. above and full name here.
4 ☐ Head of household (with qualifying person). (See page 7 of Instructions.) If the qualifying person is your child but not your dependent, enter child's name here.
5 ☐ Qualifying widow(er) with dependent child (year spouse died ▶ 19). (See page 7 of Instructions.)

Exemptions
(See Instructions on page 8.)
6a ☐ Yourself If someone (such as your parent) can claim you as a dependent on his or her tax return, do not check box 6a. But be sure to check the box on line 33b on page 2.
b ☐ Spouse
c Dependents:

(1) Name (first, initial, and last name)	(2) Check if under age 2	(3) If age 2 or older, dependent's social security number	(4) Relationship	(5) No. of months lived in your home in 1989

No. of boxes checked on 6a and 6b
No. of your children on 6c who: ● lived with you ● didn't live with you due to divorce or separation (see page 9)
No. of other dependents on 6c

d If your child didn't live with you but is claimed as your dependent under a pre-1985 agreement, check here ▶☐
e Total number of exemptions claimed ... **0**

Income
Please attach Copy B of your Forms W-2, W-2G, and W-2P here.
If you do not have a W-2, see page 6 of Instructions.

7 Wages, salaries, tips, etc. (attach Form(s) W-2) — 7
8a Taxable interest income (also attach Schedule B if over $400) — 8a
b Tax-exempt interest income (see page 10). DON'T include on line 8a. 8b
9 Dividend income (also attach Schedule B if over $400) — 9
10 Taxable refunds of state and local income taxes, if any, from worksheet on page 11 of Instructions. — 10
11 Alimony received — 11
12 Business income or (loss) (attach Schedule C). — 12 **3177**
13 Capital gain or (loss) (attach Schedule D) — 13
14 Capital gain distributions not reported on line 13 (see page 11) — 14
15 Other gains or (losses) (attach Form 4797) — 15
16a Total IRA distributions 16a 16b Taxable amount (see page 11) 16b
17a Total pensions and annuities 17a 17b Taxable amount (see page 12) 17b
18 Rents, royalties, partnerships, estates, trusts, etc. (attach Schedule E) — 18
19 Farm income or (loss) (attach Schedule F) — 19
20 Unemployment compensation (insurance) (see page 13) — 20

Please attach check or money order here.

21a Social security benefits. 21a 21b Taxable amount (see page 13) 21b
22 Other income (list type and amount—see page 13) — 22
23 Add the amounts shown in the far right column for lines 7 through 22. This is your total income ▶ 23 **3177**

Adjustments to Income
(See Instructions on page 14.)

24 Your IRA deduction, from applicable worksheet on page 14 or 15 24
25 Spouse's IRA deduction, from applicable worksheet on page 14 or 15 25
26 Self-employed health insurance deduction, from worksheet on page 15 26
27 Keogh retirement plan and self-employed SEP deduction 27
28 Penalty on early withdrawal of savings 28
29 Alimony paid. a Recipient's last name and b social security number. 29
30 Add lines 24 through 29. These are your total adjustments ▶ 30 **0**

Adjusted Gross Income
31 Subtract line 30 from line 23. This is your adjusted gross income. If this line is less than $19,340 and a child lived with you, see "Earned Income Credit" (line 58) on page 20 of the Instructions. If you want IRS to figure your tax, see page 16 of the Instructions ▶ 31 **3177**

Form 1040 (1989)   Page **2**

Tax Compu- tation	32	Amount from line 31 (adjusted gross income)	32	**3177**

33a Check if: ☐ **You** were 65 or older ☐ Blind; ☐ **Spouse** was 65 or older ☐ Blind.
   Add the number of boxes checked and enter the total here ▶ 33a

   b If someone (such as your parent) can claim you as a dependent, check here ▶ 33b ☑

   c If you are married filing a separate return and your spouse itemizes deductions,
   or you are a dual-status alien, see page 16 and check here ▶ 33c ☐

34 Enter the {• Your **standard deduction** (from page 17 of the Instructions), **OR**
   larger   • Your **itemized deductions** (from Schedule A, line 26).
   of: If you itemize, attach Schedule A and check here ▶ ☐}   34 **3100**

35 Subtract line 34 from line 32. Enter the result here 35 **77**

36 Multiply $2,000 by the total number of exemptions claimed on line 6e . 36 **—**

37 **Taxable income.** Subtract line 36 from line 35. Enter the result (if less than zero, enter zero) 37 **77**
   Caution: If under age 14 and you have more than $1,000 of investment income, check here ▶ ☐
   and see page 17 to see if you have to use Form 8615 to figure your tax.

38 Enter tax. Check if from: a ☑ Tax Table, b ☐ Tax Rate Schedules, or c ☐ Form 8615
   (If any is from Form(s) 8814, enter that amount here ▶ _____.) 38 **13**

39 Additional taxes (see page 18). Check if from: a ☐ Form 4970 b ☐ Form 4972 39 **—**

40 Add lines 38 and 39. Enter the total ....▶ 40 **13**

Credits (See Instructions on page 18.)	41	Credit for child and dependent care expenses (attach Form 2441)	41	
	42	Credit for the elderly or the disabled (attach Schedule R)	42	
	43	Foreign tax credit (attach Form 1116)	43	
	44	General business credit. Check if from: a ☐ Form 3800 or b ☐ Form (specify) _____	44	
	45	Credit for prior year minimum tax (attach Form 8801)	45	

46 Add lines 41 through 45. Enter the total 46 **0**

47 Subtract line 46 from line 40. Enter the result (if less than zero, enter zero) ▶ 47 **13**

Other Taxes (Including Advance EIC Payments)	48	Self-employment tax (attach Schedule SE)	48	**414**
	49	Alternative minimum tax (attach Form 6251)	49	
	50	Recapture taxes (see page 18). Check if from: a ☐ Form 4255 b ☐ Form 8611	50	
	51	Social security tax on tip income not reported to employer (attach Form 4137)	51	
	52	Tax on an IRA or a qualified retirement plan (attach Form 5329)	52	
	53	Add lines 47 through 52. Enter the total ▶	53	**427**

Medicare Premium	54	Supplemental Medicare premium (attach Form 8808)	54	
	55	Add lines 53 and 54. This is your **total tax** and any supplemental Medicare premium ▶	55	**427**

Payments Attach Forms W-2, W-2G, and W-2P to front.	56	Federal income tax withheld (if any is from Form(s) 1099, check ▶ ☐)	56	
	57	1989 estimated tax payments and amount applied from 1988 return	57	
	58	Earned income credit (see page 20)	58	
	59	Amount paid with Form 4868 (extension request)	59	
	60	Excess social security tax and RRTA tax withheld (see page 20)	60	
	61	Credit for Federal tax on fuels (attach Form 4136)	61	
	62	Regulated investment company credit (attach Form 2439)	62	
	63	Add lines 56 through 62. These are your **total payments** ▶	63	**0**

Refund or Amount You Owe	64	If line 63 is larger than line 55, enter amount **OVERPAID** ▶	64	
	65	Amount of line 64 to be **REFUNDED TO YOU** ▶	65	
	66	Amount of line 64 to be **APPLIED TO YOUR 1990 ESTIMATED TAX** ▶ 66		
	67	If line 55 is larger than line 63, enter **AMOUNT YOU OWE.** Attach check or money order for full amount payable to "Internal Revenue Service." Write your social security number, daytime phone number, and "1989 Form 1040" on it	67	**427**
	68	Penalty for underpayment of estimated tax (see page 21)	68	

Sign Here
(Keep a copy of this return for your records.)

Under penalties of perjury, I declare that I have examined this return and accompanying schedules and statements, and to the best of my knowledge and belief, they are true, correct, and complete. Declaration of preparer (other than taxpayer) is based on all information of which preparer has any knowledge.

Your signature	Date	Your occupation
Amanda J. Keller	1-15-90	**Self-employed**
Spouse's signature (if joint return, BOTH must sign)	Date	Spouse's occupation

Paid Preparer's Use Only

Preparer's signature		Date	Check if self-employed ☐	Preparer's social security no.
Firm's name (or yours if self-employed) and address			E.I. No.	
			ZIP code	

☼U.S.G.P.O. 1989-245-447/448/449/519 E.I. 43-0787287

SCHEDULE C (Form 1040) Department of the Treasury Internal Revenue Service (O)	**Profit or Loss From Business** (Sole Proprietorship) **Partnerships, Joint Ventures, Etc., Must File Form 1065.** ▶ Attach to Form 1040 or Form 1041. ▶ See Instructions for Schedule C (Form 1040).	OMB No. 1545-0074 **1989** Attachment Sequence No. 09

Name of proprietor		Social security number (SSN)
Amanda J. Keller		**483 123 4567**

A Principal business or profession, including product or service (see Instructions) **House Cleaning**

B Principal business code (from page 2) ▶ **7 4 7 6**

C Business name and address ▶ ...... **Housecare**
..... **#20 Oak Grove – Decatur, IL 01234** ....

D Employer ID number (Not SSN)

E Method(s) used to value closing inventory: (1) ☐ Cost (2) ☐ Lower of cost or market (3) ☐ Other (attach explanation) (4) ☐ Does not apply (if checked, skip line G)

		Yes	No
F Accounting method: (1) ☑ Cash (2) ☐ Accrual (3) ☐ Other (specify) ▶			
G Was there any change in determining quantities, costs, or valuations between opening and closing inventory? (If "Yes," attach explanation.)			✓
H Are you deducting expenses for business use of your home? (If "Yes," see Instructions for limitations.)			✓
I Did you "materially participate" in the operation of this business during 1989? (If "No," see Instructions for limitations on losses.)		✓	

J If this schedule is a loss, credit, deduction, income, or any other tax benefit relating to a tax shelter required to be registered, check here . ▶ ☐
If you checked this box, you MUST attach **Form 8271.**

Part I Income

1	Gross receipts or sales	1	**3400**	
2	Returns and allowances	2	—	
3	Subtract line 2 from line 1. Enter the result here		3	**3400**
4	Cost of goods sold and/or operations (from line 39 on page 2)		4	—
5	Subtract line 4 from line 3 and enter the **gross profit** here		5	**3400**
6	Other income, including Federal and state gasoline or fuel tax credit or refund (see Instructions)		6	—
7	Add lines 5 and 6. This is your **gross income** ▶		7	**3400**

Part II Expenses

8	Advertising	8	**20**	22 Repairs	22	**98**
9	Bad debts from sales or services (see Instructions)	9		23 Supplies (not included in Part III)	23	
10	Car and truck expenses	10		24 Taxes	24	
11	Commissions	11		25 Travel, meals, and entertainment:		
12	Depletion	12		a Travel	25a	
13	Depreciation and section 179 deduction from **Form 4562** (not included in Part III)	13		b Meals and entertainment		
14	Employee benefit programs (other than on line 20)	14		c Enter 20% of line 25b subject to limitations (see Instructions)		
15	Freight (not included in Part III)	15		d Subtract line 25c from line 25b	25d	
16	Insurance (other than health)	16		26 Utilities (see Instructions)	26	
17	Interest:			27 Wages (less jobs credit)	27	
a	Mortgage (paid to banks, etc.)	17a		28 Other expenses (list type and amount):		
b	Other	17b		...... **Uniform** 20		
18	Legal and professional services	18		...... **Bank fees** 60		
19	Office expense	19	**25**			
20	Pension and profit-sharing plans	20				
21	Rent or lease:					
a	Machinery and equipment	21a				
b	Other business property	21b		28		**80**

29	Add amounts in columns for lines 8 through 28. These are your **total expenses** ▶	29	**223**
30	Net profit or (loss). Subtract line 29 from line 7. If a profit, enter here and on Form 1040, line 12, and on Schedule SE, line 2. If a loss, you MUST go on to line 31. (Fiduciaries, see Instructions.)	30	**3177**

31 If you have a loss, you MUST check the box that describes your investment in this activity (see Instructions) . . . .   31a ☐ All investment is at risk.
If you checked 31a, enter the loss on Form 1040, line 12, and Schedule SE, line 2.   31b ☐ Some investment is not at risk.
If you checked 31b, you MUST attach **Form 6198.**

For Paperwork Reduction Act Notice, see Form 1040 Instructions.   Schedule C (Form 1040) 1989

SCHEDULE SE	**Social Security Self-Employment Tax**	OMB No. 1545-0074
(Form 1040)	▶ See Instructions for Schedule SE (Form 1040).	1989
Department of the Treasury Internal Revenue Service (O)	▶ Attach to Form 1040.	Attachment Sequence No. 18

Name of person with **self-employment** income (as shown on social security card) Amanda J. Keller	Social security number of person with **self-employment** income ▶	483 123 4567

Who Must File Schedule SE

You must file Schedule SE if:

- Your net earnings from self-employment were $400 or more (or you had wages of $100 or more from an electing church or church-controlled organization); AND
- Your wages (subject to social security or railroad retirement tax) were less than $48,000.

Exception. If your only self-employment income was from earnings as a minister, member of a religious order, or Christian Science practitioner, AND you filed **Form 4361** and received IRS approval not to be taxed on those earnings, DO NOT file Schedule SE. Instead, write "Exempt–Form 4361" on Form 1040, line 48.

For more information about Schedule SE, see the Instructions.

Note: *Most people can use the short Schedule SE on this page. But, you may have to use the longer Schedule SE that is on the back.*

Who MUST Use the Long Schedule SE (Section B)

You must use Section B if ANY of the following applies:

- You choose the "optional method" to figure your self-employment tax (see Section B, Part II);
- You are a minister, member of a religious order, or Christian Science practitioner and you received IRS approval (from **Form 4361**) not to be taxed on your earnings from these sources, but you owe self-employment tax on other earnings;
- You were an employee of a church or church-controlled organization that chose by law not to pay employer social security taxes;
- You had tip income that is subject to social security tax, but you did not report those tips to your employer; OR
- You were a government employee with wages subject ONLY to the 1.45% Medicare part of the social security tax.

Section A—Short Schedule SE
(Read above to see if you must use the long Schedule SE on the back (Section B).)

1	Net farm profit or (loss) from Schedule F (Form 1040), line 36, and farm partnerships, Schedule K-1 (Form 1065), line 14a	1	
2	Net profit or (loss) from Schedule C (Form 1040), line 30, and Schedule K-1 (Form 1065), line 14a (other than farming). See the Instructions for other income to report	2	3177
3	Add lines 1 and 2. Enter the total. If the total is less than $400, **do not** file this schedule; you **do not** owe self-employment tax ▶	3	3177
4	The largest amount of combined wages and self-employment earnings subject to social security or railroad retirement tax (tier 1) for 1989 is	4	$48,000 00
5	Total social security wages and tips (from Form(s) W-2) and railroad retirement compensation (tier 1)	5	0
6	Subtract line 5 from line 4. Enter the result. If the result is zero or less, stop here; you **do not** owe self-employment tax ▶	6	48,000
7	Enter the **smaller** of line 3 or line 6	7	3177
8	Rate of tax	8	×.1302
9	**Self-employment tax.** If line 7 is $48,000, enter $6,249.60. Otherwise, multiply the amount on line 7 by the decimal amount on line 8 and enter the result. Also enter this amount on Form 1040, line 48	9	414

For Paperwork Reduction Act Notice, see Form 1040 Instructions.   Schedule SE (Form 1040) 1989

Estimated Tax

One complication for the small business owner is the requirement for you to pay "Estimated Tax." If you are an employee of a company, you know that your employer regularly withholds tax from your paycheck and sends that to the government for you. Normally, by the end of the year, your tax obligation has already been paid in full. Payment of Estimated Tax for you is like having an employer withhold taxes on a paycheck. The government wants you to pay your taxes as you go along, rather than wait until the end of the year.

How do you know if you need to pay Estimated Tax during the year? The government requires you to make tax payments during the year, before your annual tax return is due, IF you estimate that you'll owe at least $500 in taxes by year-end. This $500 is a combination of income and self-employment taxes. For the 1989 tax year, you could have earned $3,450 before your tax obligation exceeded $500. Your library or local IRS office will have a copy of Form 1040-ES, Estimated Tax for Individuals. It explains the rules and payment schedules for filing.

Index